Personal Magic

For more information on readings or workshops, visit

www.jenniemarlow.com

or email information@jenniemarlow.com

Personal Magic

◆

Creating Life, Love, and Work That Resonate with Your Soul

*A Spotted Eagle &
Grandfather White Elk Book
Channeled by Jennie Marlow*

iUniverse, Inc.
New York Lincoln Shanghai

Personal Magic
Creating Life, Love, and Work That Resonate with Your Soul

iUniverse, Inc.

For information address:
iUniverse, Inc.
2021 Pine Lake Road, Suite 100
Lincoln, NE 68512
www.iuniverse.com

ISBN: 0-595-29318-2

Printed in the United States of America

To my husband and soulmate

Contents

Introduction xi

Overcoming Fear 1

Expanding Your Awareness of What is Possible. 7
    Meditation for Entering the Field of All Possibility. 7
    Meditation for Releasing Unwanted Thoughts & Feelings 9
    Meditation for Changing the Matrix of Your Thought-Forms 10

Being in Present Time. 13
    Meditation for Examining Your Life. 15
    Exercise for Identifying Judgments & Fears About Your Circumstances 16
    Meditation for Releasing Judgment & Fear. 17

The Essence & Form of What You Desire. 18
    Exercise for Identifying the Essence of What You Want to Create 19
    Meditation for Transmuting Fear into Desire. 23
    Exercise for Seeing Essence You Already Have 24

Actualizing the Possibilities 26
    Exercise for Describing the Life of Your Dreams. 26

Purpose & Intention 30
    Exercise for Life Purpose, Part 1 31
    Exercise for Life Purpose, Part 2 32

Vision 35
    Exercise for Describing Vision & Identifying Essence 35

Being Your Authentic Self. 42

Stalkers and Dreamers 44

Personal Magic 51

- *Time Mastery* 52
- *Sex Magic* 57
- *Void Traveling* 60
- *Stillness Magic* 65
- *Phoenix Magic* 70
- *Illumination Magic* 74
- *Healing Touch* 78
- *Sacred Weaving* 82

Co-creating Your Life with Spirit 86

    Meditation for Creating with Personal Magic 89

APPENDIX   Essence Words 95

Acknowledgments

I would like to thank Kathleen Sims, President of Certain Solutions in Concord, California, for teaching me her wonderful work on vision and purpose, and for the enormous contribution her work made to all of the written exercises in this book. Charles Davies receives my heartfelt thanks for his unflagging encouragement and the many hours he spent with me while I channeled information from Spotted Eagle and Grandfather White Elk. I want to thank Rob Robb for giving me permission to speak my truth, and Judith Star Medicine for introducing me to Spotted Eagle. I would also like to give special thanks to Judy Fuson for mentoring me through the process of becoming a professional psychic.

Thanks to my wonderful editors, Gerry Connolly and Emily Fox, and to others whose contribution to the manuscript has been enormously helpful: Maggie Self, Peter Matthies, Jules Wittrup, Steve Hertzog and Jennifer Hathaway.

My deepest appreciation and gratitude is given to Spotted Eagle and Grandfather White Elk for transforming my life and for offering me the priceless gift of their wisdom, teachings, and companionship.

And finally, I want to thank my Dreaming Time Master husband and soulmate, Phil, for his boundless love and for his support of all my outlandish endeavors as a Stalking Phoenix Magic.

Introduction

I have walked the road of self-improvement for most of my adult life. Years of psychotherapy, workshops, and intensives seemed to take me only so far. I studied astrology and tarot, consulted healers and psychics, and trained to become a channel of spirit guides. All of these efforts were partially successful, but in each an every case, I would hit an inevitable wall where the principles failed to bring about a permanent shift from struggle to flow. In almost twenty years as a corporate executive, I attempted to put into practice what I knew to be spiritually correct, but I could never seem to achieve a functioning partnership between material life and spirituality.

I began channeling for the first time almost fifteen years ago. Over the intervening years, scores of guides have come to teach me about the universe and lead me along my path. When I reached a certain level of skill in what my guides imparted to me, my group would undergo a change. As each group departed to make way for the next, I felt both sadness and exhilaration because this transition always meant that new information and a spurt of growth would soon be forthcoming. Reading for friends was very rewarding, but I could not imagine that I would ever be a professional psychic. My path seemed clearly charted in the corporate world as an entrepreneur, manager, and consultant.

When I was first introduced to Spotted Eagle, I was standing in the wreckage of a thirteen-year period of failure that had cost me my first marriage, three businesses, my home, and almost everything I owned. My health was declining rapidly, and it was clear that I was at a crossroads. While my prospects were not encouraging, it seemed to me that I had opened an enormous space in my life for something, but I had no idea what that something might be.

Spotted Eagle put my entire life in context in a single conversation. When he told me about my personal magic, issues I had grappled with for years suddenly made perfect sense. I could see so clearly that I had spent my entire life trying to express Phoenix Magic, in one form or another, but I had been unconscious of what was motivating me to do so. Within a few weeks of my first conversation with him, Spotted Eagle began to visit me occasionally in my meditations. I noticed that my meditations were taking a whole new track, and that the images he was showing me had very deep symbolic meanings. Soon it was clear that

Spotted Eagle was helping me to bring about an entirely new vision for my life's work.

A few months after I was introduced to Spotted Eagle, my husband and I made a pilgrimage to the places that Spotted Eagle said he loved in Wyoming and South Dakota. He had instructed me to be guided and led, and he promised me that when I found what I was there for, he would send me a sign.

The day we discovered Bear Butte it was hot and muggy, and the place was full of tourists. Native Americans who were plainly there to carry out their spiritual practices cast disparaging glances at the shirtless and scantily clad Whites who were traipsing all over their sacred shrine. I felt uncomfortable, as if I were intruding. But this had been a Lakota shrine for hundreds of years, and I knew that I was on ground that Spotted Eagle had surely walked. I wanted to hike the trail up to the top of the butte to honor him, so we started out. It was not long before the heat took its toll. People were passing us on the trail, and I was beginning to realize that I was not fit enough to complete the climb. My husband kept assuring me that getting to the top was not critical. I remember turning to him and asking, "Are you sure?"

It was then that Grandfather White Elk made himself known to me for the very first time. He said, "It is only important if you are here to conquer the mountain. If you are here to worship, then getting to the top is of no importance." His words made me weep. I knew they were words to live by. Later, when we were away from the crowds and having our lunch in the shade of the trees at the foot of Bear Butte, Spotted Eagle delivered on his promise. I looked up at the mountain just as four eagles were flying into view. They circled overhead, and then they were gone.

This was the start of the most rich and rewarding period of my life. When I opened to channel these two extraordinary beings, I honestly had no idea where it would lead. Now it is not a question that even concerns me because where they take me day-to-day is the most interesting and enjoyable place I have ever been. It is an honor to be one of their channels, but more than that, I feel I have developed friendships that will take me through this life and beyond. The enormous space I had opened in my life is now filled with channeling and teaching what Spotted Eagle and Grandfather White Elk want to contribute to those whose lives they touch.

This is a book about finding self as Spotted Eagle and Grandfather White Elk define it. They teach that each one of us is born with gifts of Spirit, and it is through the use of these gifts that we manifest the highest good for ourselves, for others, and for the world. They call these gifts *personal magic*. Magic could be defined as the art of influencing events, and it is certainly that. Perhaps more importantly, personal magic is about being our authentic selves. It is about using the power of this authenticity to create opportunities, relationships and yes, even material resources, all in the service of higher good.

It is easy to forget that we are part of Creation. Whenever we think about the universe, how often do we recognize that we are speaking about something that *includes* us? If you chose to open this book, you are probably already aware that you have a connection to Spirit. What you are only beginning to glimpse is the potential that this relationship has for co-creating your life.

In the pages that follow, you will read the teachings of Spotted Eagle and Grandfather White Elk. They explain how the universe works, how creation-events occur, and how we can shift our energy to make creating things more effortless. The meditations are also theirs. The written exercises were inspired by the work of one of my most influential teachers, Kathleen Sims, whose teachings about vision and purpose continue to change my life.

This book is meant to be a kind of textbook for the principles of creating with personal magic. The exercises and meditations are presented in a sequence that will assist you in examining your blocks to creativity, releasing them, and creating from a new place of joy and ease.

I wish you an enlightening and meaningful journey.

Jennie Marlow

Overcoming Fear

When you were born, you lived in present time with no thought beyond your immediate needs and desires. As you matured, concerns about the future and your ability to command resources began to replace the trust you once had that your needs would be met. For some of you, this happened quite early in childhood.

You may not be aware of how much thought-energy you invest in trying to make your future predictable. You may not realize the degree to which worrying about the future affects your perception of yourself, your life, and your potential. If you have a strong need for security, you may find that you have sacrificed many of your hopes and dreams to your fears about the future.

It is easy to see that most suffering you undergo is self-induced as a result of fear, even though most of the things you fear never come to pass. For most of you, physical suffering and tragedy are rare events that occasionally occur as part of every human life. But if you examine the focus of your thinking, you will discover that you spend most of your waking moments thinking the same fear-based thoughts you had the day before, indeed for most of the days of your life. You have come to live with fear as a constant companion, always there, never failing to encourage you to feel unsafe, powerless, and unlovable.

It is not difficult to recognize that fear is at the root of the anger, violence, greed, and exploitation that plague your world. But in an even more immediate sense, fear is the energy that blocks your creativity, clouds your vision, and stops you from moving in the direction of your dreams. If you let it, your fear will make you feel needy and victimized. It will even prompt you to avoid life or compel you to try to control, manipulate, and dominate others. In those areas where you have given fear dominion, you have no choice but to squander your life force in a futile attempt to run from fear or try to prevent what you fear from happening.

The part of you that harbors fears about the future craves more than anything to feel as if it has control of the outcome of things in order to feel more secure. But since there really is no way to be absolutely secure, fear will always creep in through the cracks of whatever measures you take to control the outcomes of your life or what you call the *future.*

The truth is there is no future except the one you have created with your imagination. Sure, events will come to pass. Some things will go on as they have always done, new things will be created, and some things will pass away. But the future you worry about is not real. If it was real, then everything you imagine about it would eventually manifest. Clearly it does not, and considering how many fears you conjure up, and the creativity you employ in refining the details, this is probably a good thing!

The future you imagine is manufactured by the part of you that is afraid and tries to find ways to get relief from that fear. Your belief in a future is partly a function of the past. Because that past appeared to be created in the progress of time, it may have led you to believe this is evidence of the existence of a future, already formed, that is moving toward you along that same progression. In this way, you have become convinced of the existence of a future, one that can be controlled to create the outcome that will make you the least afraid. It is this fearful part of you that we call *Mind.*

Where did Mind originate? The easiest answer might be found by studying anthropology and the conditions under which *Homo sapiens* evolved. Survival of the individual depended upon survival of the tribal group. The social tools that human beings used to keep groups together—rejection, blame, rescuing, shame, and guilt—were essential to physical survival. Under these conditions, fear of the future held groups together and helped them cooperate to ensure the survival of individuals whose chances would be slim if left on their own.

Conditions have changed dramatically over the course of millennia, and your physical survival no longer depends upon these negative emotions. However, Mind has not evolved to meet the circumstances of modern life. Instead it has taken what it knows about physical survival in a wilderness of life-threatening conditions and has applied it to your emotions, turning them into matters of life and death. Threats to survival are all Mind is capable of knowing. It views everything it experiences through a filter defined by its measurement of perceived control over events, people, and conditions. When you give Mind dominion over your emotions, it is impossible to be in present time because Mind knows only what it fears, and Mind's fears are always about the future it seeks to control.

Mind believes in what it fears. This makes Mind an expert at debating, and because its belief is so strong, it will ultimately win any argument. This is why affirmations often fail to work, especially if they allow Mind to hide beneath the positive statements you lay over the top of what you fear, thereby obscuring it.

An aware person, someone who is conscious of his or her feelings, has an irresistible impulse to argue with the fears Mind presents. This effort might be temporarily successful, but when one does not have dominion over Mind, then Mind will eventually erode the defense of that argument by coming up with a new fearful scenario against which the argument has no power. This is why your culture looks for facts and proof. They make you feel less afraid of uncertainty and trick you into believing that, with more evidence, you can win your argument with Mind.

Mind prefers to operate in the shadows at unconscious levels. Unsupervised, Mind can wreak havoc on your psyche, carrying you away on a flight of fearful fancy. This journey into imagined fears can preoccupy you so completely that you leave present time and come to live in your imaginary future or your regrettable past, a world composed of scenarios of what Mind fears. Then you set about trying to create a life built upon preventing or surviving what Mind fears will come to pass. You become hyper-vigilant, fueling the imaginary multiplicity of things to fight or avoid.

Mind has trained you to think, not in terms of what you truly desire, but in the context of what you do not want. When this focus on what you fear is the foundation of what you create, the life you want in your heart is very hard to come by. The reason is simple: when you fear, the doors to the Creator are slammed shut by your neediness, attachment, and preoccupation with control, where only the rigid outcome designed by your fear will suit you.

Mind actually does have a useful side. It is very good at discerning things, like telling you whether or not it is safe to cross the street in traffic. It lets you know you are uncomfortable with something that is going on around you, prompting you to pay closer attention and determine if there is a danger. It signals the body to respond to danger, and it can learn and remember what threatened it in the past so that it can be more responsive to similar threats, should they arise again.

Mind has legitimate needs for power, safety, and value. When Mind is enlightened, it knows how to meet these needs through cooperation with Spirit. But when you allow Mind to go unsupervised—when you give it dominion over your emotions—it gives emotional threats the same importance as physical ones. The body reacts with a stress response that makes the threat seem all the more real, as if it were a danger to your physical survival. And so the fear feeds on itself, ultimately increasing Mind's power. If we are to claim our birthright of joy, creativity, and ease, we must give Spirit dominion over Mind.

When Spirit has dominion over Mind, Mind flourishes in a healthy state, like an organ of the body that is fully functioning. By moving your consciousness into present time, Mind's fear of the future has no context in which to operate. It is thereby restored to the function for which it was intended, to keep you out of harm's way and help you manage the natural ebb and flow of resources available to you.

We are all invited to co-create with the Creator and make our lives a beautiful dance of joy. Mind can actually help you in this effort. When you feel fear, it is a signal that you are not in the moment. When you learn to use fear as a reminder that you are not in present time—that you are not in touch with what you desire most in that moment—you can respond by returning your attention to your heart center and the desires that you hold there. In this way Mind can become a welcome partner in your co-creation with Spirit.

Your soul is like a cell in the body of the Creator. It is a living, evolving expression of divinity. It is individual, with its own form and function, and yet an integral part of the Creator. You are a child of the Creator, a small part of all that is. Likewise, only a small part of your soul is engaged in the human experience you call your life. Just as you yourself have many activities and vehicles for expression, so does your soul, and inhabiting your body and living your life is only one of those activities. When you, as your soul, decided to engage in a human experience, you did so with the intention of overcoming fear and evolving Mind. In some lives you fulfilled your intention and in others you may have been less successful. If you choose, you are given as many opportunities as you want in order to complete your evolutionary process. When you understand that the purpose of every soul is to evolve fear into love, you can see why living a human is life is so valuable and appealing, in spite of its tribulations.

Everything in the universe is on a journey that is leading inexorably toward its own higher evolution. The evolutionary force that makes this possible has within it all the tools necessary for transformation. Chief among them is free will. This means it is up to the individual to choose how to react to events and people, to choose what to believe and to take action based upon that belief. Because of free will, you define the route by which your own evolution is progressing. Once you are born into the body, free will is the way you make the choices that lead up to events, circumstances, and relationships by which you will evolve. When you choose a particularly difficult path or one that is not heading in the direction of your evolution, your soul has to put a great deal of energy into getting you to course-correct. It will do this by summoning people and events that encourage you to become aware of what you are doing and prompt you to make a needed change. What you experience can be upsetting or make you feel like you have had a terrible setback. It can create a period of stasis where nothing seems to be happening, despite all of your strenuous efforts.

When you are following the course dictated by the fearful Mind, your soul's energy will be directed toward getting you to wake up and surrender your ego attachment to whatever it is you are pursuing. Your soul will increasingly put pressure on you to stop what you are doing and examine your beliefs about reality. The discomfort you feel is Spirit signaling you that you are ready to resolve whatever issue is keeping you from living in the moment.

Fear is the only emotion that pulls you away from the now. Conquering fear requires discipline. This discipline is an exercise in awareness, in recognizing fear as it arises and not allowing it to carry you off into your projections.

You are most vulnerable to Mind when something in your life changes, especially if that change makes you uncertain about what comes next. The uncertainty shatters your illusion that the future is knowable. It reminds you of the cosmic truth that the future is nothing but unformed potential, and if you allow fear to rise in this moment, Mind seizes power over your awareness and robs you of dominion over time.

When you lose dominion over time and start projecting your fears out into the future, this product of your imagination will become your reality. Recall a fear that you commonly have. Notice how your body feels when you give this fear attention. Take a few deep breaths and consciously enter the present moment. Notice the transformation in the way your body feels.

The breath is your best technique to bring you to and anchor you in the moment. This is because the breath has dominion over time. The breath is your interface with the Creator who has filled the field all around you with energy, and as you breathe it in, you become aligned and fully present in the moment. This allows you to confront fear and face it for what it is: not a powerful enemy, but a pathetic and weak illusion. When you see the spiritual truth, fear loses all power. You know instinctively not to fight with something that is not real, and you are no longer compelled to waste your energy in that way. You can then begin even to find humor in the fear, to find lightness of being and have compassion for yourself. When you do this the fear dissolves.

Present time is your access to transformation. It holds within it a context for living wherein there is no future to avoid and no past to repeat or change. By acknowledging that there is no future the way you used to think about it, you can stop wanting or counting on things to happen a certain way. You can acknowledge that this is really only your neediness for security. When you surrender your need to know what the future will be, you can throw open the door to the soul and allow the Creator to dance with you—to be spontaneous with you—and restore you to your birthright: a life filled with joy, creativity, and ease.

Expanding Your Awareness of What is Possible

We in the higher dimensions know the material plane to be a field of space-time in a state of constant transformation. All of this occurs in the unbroken infinity we call the universe: the Creator expressed as Creation, composed of energy and form in the eternal present moment. This eternal present moment—or *present time*—carries within it the unlimited potential of the universe. Creation is not only what has been created, it is also the unlimited potential for what will be. It is a boundless continuum of energies, completely interconnected, like a fabric whose threads intersect in an infinite number of dimensions. We refer to these energies in present time as the *void*, not because it is empty, but because it is the unformed potential of all that will be created as the universe evolves.

Meditation for Entering the Field of All Possibility

Close your eyes. Take a few deep, rhythmic breaths to bring yourself into the moment. When you feel relaxed, imagine there is a portal, and when you walk through it, you enter the void, the field of all possibility. See or sense the unlimited potential from which everything is formed. Notice that the void is filled with the energy of infinite possibilities, and that as you remain here, your awareness of these possibilities begins to expand. Realize that the energies contained in the void are something that you can travel upon or just observe, as you choose. Recognize that in spite of its infinite potential, the void is not something in which you could ever lose yourself because the only activity you can perform within it is to expand your awareness of what is possible. Spend as much time as you like exploring and observing the infinite potential of the universe in present time.

If you find you cannot move into the void, examine what Mind may be telling you. Living in present time is not about standing outside of the doorway to the void and worrying about the uncertainty that the field of all possibility implies.

That is *fear* of the void. This fear—the fear of uncertainty—may cause you to remain in the dominion of Mind and not walk through the portal. On Mind's side of the portal, Mind will look into the void and see emptiness, isolation, or total abandonment. These are a reflection of whatever your core issues may be. If you do not cross the threshold, Mind will heighten your fear by predicting that the void contains within it great potential for negative things or for nothing at all. Living with uncertainty in present time—embracing the void—is the best way to shut down Mind's fearful influence over you. Bring the void into your everyday existence, and live within the truth of its marvelous spontaneity and invitation to adventure.

Present time is the reality of the cosmos. The act of creating begins by bringing all the potential of the universe in present time into your awareness with the determination to ground your consciousness there. The cosmic reality is this: there are an infinite number of possible outcomes at any given point in space-time. The art is in entering the void, expanding your awareness of the possibilities, and actualizing the one you choose.

There really is no future as you have come to think of it. What creates events that will come to pass is a construct of energy that might best be described as a *matrix*. Some matrices are so fixed that they become more or less predictable, like the earth's rotation that causes the sun to appear to rise and set. Because there are matrices that seem predictable, you think of the future as something that actually exists in the sense that it might be formed and foretold. This is not the case. In the eternal now, there is only what has already been created and the unlimited potential for what will be.

Everything in Creation has consciousness. Your physicists have discovered that photons, particle-waves of light, appear to know instantaneously what other photons are doing, even over distances so vast they are almost unimaginable. You might be surprised to learn that the very act of observing subatomic particles affects their behavior. Both of these discoveries are demonstrations that everything in Creation has some form of thought, and it is these very thought-forms that make up the matrix of Creation. This matrix of thought-forms gives birth to what will be, from the totality of the universe down to its most minute subatomic particle.

Your thoughts are forms of energy. If you notice, they actually do have a life of their own. Once you birth them into being they seem to operate independently of consciousness. This is because, when you think the same thought over and over again, you add substance to the thought and make it a part of your own unique matrix of thought-forms. Your matrix is woven inextricably with the universal matrix of which it is a part. But more importantly, your matrix constitutes your literal agreement with the Creator about what your reality will be and how you will affect the universe. This reality is composed not only of your perceptions, but also what you are destined to attract by way of experience, people, events, and even possessions.

If you are to change your reality, you must start at the level of your thoughts. Your imagination is what creates any thoughts you have about the future. The fears in your imagination are what built the part of your matrix that is creating most of your suffering. And you can use that same tool—your imagination—to deconstruct what is limiting you and then rebuild it.

The task of changing your matrix begins by preventing thoughts and feelings you do not want from adding more substance to the thought-forms that are already there. You can do this simply by releasing the energy of your thoughts and feelings into the void, returning that energy to the unmanifested potential of the universe, thus allowing the energy of your thoughts and feelings to evolve on their own higher path.

Do this eyes-open meditation throughout the day, every time you are aware that a thought or feeling is making you uncomfortable.

Meditation for Releasing Unwanted Thoughts & Feelings

Take a very deep breath and, in your imagination, walk through a portal and into the void, the field of all possibility. Invite the thought and your reaction to it into the void to be released to their higher evolution.

We often tell those of you who find your way to us that we have never met a thought or a feeling that did not want to be released to its higher evolution. This is because, at their most basic level, thoughts are forms of energy, and all energy wants to follow the Creator's design. This design is the force which ensures that everything in the universe evolves. When you make a fear-based thought or feeling part of your matrix, you trap the energy, thereby working against the Creator's design. The ensuing suffering you experience is really a prompting by Spirit to release that thought or feeling and evolve your matrix.

When you were born, your matrix had within it all the agreements you had made before entering this life. Some of these agreements were with important people in your life: parents, siblings, partners, your children and your friends, just to name a few. Other agreements had to do with what sorts of experiences you meant to attract to yourself in order to create the opportunities for growth that your soul was attempting to fulfill in this lifetime. When you were an infant, most of your matrix was designed to provide you with instinctive behavior, and also with the desire for mobility and communication. Your matrix prepared you to unconditionally love your caregiver. The parents you chose and the events you attracted, all of these were designed by your soul to provide a challenge to assist you in evolving beyond the fear that dominates your world. Every time you added a fear-based thought or emotion to your matrix, the result was discomfort. If you did not pay attention to this message from Spirit, Mind grew in strength and began to seduce you with its most powerful tool: worry.

Your imagination fashioned what you have added to your matrix since your birth, and it did this under the supervision of Mind. This is how powerful a role your imagination plays in the quality of your life experience. It has the ability to transport you to higher consciousness or to lock you in a prison of illusion.

The illusion of projected fear severs awareness from your life where it is actually being lived, in the here and now. When you acknowledge that there is no future—that there is *only* the eternal present moment—you reclaim your consciousness from the future imagined by Mind. When you are in present time, you automatically enter the field of all possibility where the Creator resides and where Creation stands poised to actualize potential. When you are in present time, you have access to the inspiration, love, and compassion that are built into Creation. In the field of all possibility, where there is no future to fear, and Spirit has dominion over Mind.

When you set about the task of altering the matrix, you need to engage Spirit in deconstructing the matrix and creating new thought-forms. If you want to create a life that reflects your divinity, the new thought-forms you create in place of those you deconstruct must be based on your soul's three fundamental desires: the desire for joy, creativity, and ease. This means you can, in meditation, release your fear-based thought-forms and reconstruct the matrix until it is composed entirely from the soul's desires.

Meditation for Changing the Matrix of Your Thought-Forms

Take a deep breath. Enter the field of all possibility and invite all limiting thoughts and feelings into the void to be released to their higher evolution. Imagine that you can see or sense your matrix. Imagine you are traveling along the matrix until you come to the part that is creating an area of your life that you would like to shift. Invite the thought-forms in this area to deconstruct and be released to their higher evolution. See or sense the thought-forms collapsing into dust and blowing away into the void. Feel or sense the wind of Spirit carrying away the energy of this old, fear-based thinking. In the empty space left by this deconstruction, imagine that you are creating new structures of thought from your soul's desire for joy, creativity, and ease. If you would like to work on another issue, repeat the process by finding that part of the matrix where the issue is held. When you are finished, send a request to the Ascended Masters, asking them to enlighten your mind's need for power, safety, and value.

This request of the Ascended Masters is always answered, so pause a moment and feel the subtle response by the Ascended Masters as they shift the energy of Mind within your entire body.

Daily work on your matrix should only take a few minutes, perhaps in the morning before you get out of bed or some other quiet place in your day. You will know what area to work on by the patterns you notice in what you are taking to the void throughout the day. Because fears tend to run in tracks, the theme of the thought-forms that need deconstructing is usually fairly obvious. If it is not, use the time to work on the matrix in a pro-active way, going after an area of your life that you would like to shift to a greater level of resonance.

Each day as you begin working on your matrix, notice how it looks or feels. Take a moment to sense any changes that the previous day's work might have created. It is important to notice the difference, visually or energetically, between the new matrix you have created from the soul's desires and the old matrix formed by your fear-based thoughts. Eventually the matrix as a whole will begin to have an entirely new look and feel. You will be able to notice that it is more open, dynamic, and beautiful. You will begin to feel the new level of resonance you are establishing by the work you are doing.

In a few days, you will notice that your outer reality is beginning to shift. Remember that this is a process similar to an archeological excavation: it scrapes away the issue you are working on, layer-by-layer. You will know to stop working on this area of the matrix when the issue is not showing up in your life. If it reappears, this simply means that it is time to work on the issue at a deeper level.

As you work on the matrix, you are changing your agreement with the universe about what your reality will be. Every time you deconstruct a thought-form and create a new one from your soul's desires, you are actually making a new agreement with the universe! As the matrix is reconstructed from the soul's desires, it begins to resonate with the soul, and what the matrix creates begins to shift toward this resonance. With each shift in resonance, your matrix becomes a more accurate reflection of who you are as Spirit, and this authenticity increases the potential that you are able to actualize from the field of all possibility.

Who are the Ascended Masters? And why do we make this request of them?

The Ascended Masters are those beings whose evolution has lifted their energy to a level where it has the power to speak the Creator's truth. White Buffalo Calf Lady, Lao Tse, Abraham, Jesus, the Buddha, and Mohamed are a few of the Ascended Masters with whom you might be familiar. This vast group of beings has a single purpose, and that is to enlighten Mind in the universe. An ascended master evolves Mind through the transmission of the energy of compassion. When you make a request to enlighten your own Mind, this request is always granted at whatever level you are ready to receive. It is the force of this divine compassion that creates shifts in the universal consciousness and makes possible the evolution of fear into love.

Being in Present Time

Present time includes all of the current circumstances of your life. These circumstances and the matrix that created them are part of all that is, the universe as it exists in this moment, poised to actualize from its unlimited potential. Your circumstances—the conditions, people and things in your life—are part of what has been created in the universe. To struggle, fight against, or run away from your circumstances is quite literally resisting the universe.

It is exhausting and frustrating to resist what has already been created. And it is this resistance that is causing much of your suffering. For many of you, Mind has convinced you that acceptance of your current circumstances would be like giving up, that it would plunge you into hopelessness. You may fear that accepting what is might make all your efforts up to this point a waste of time, energy, and resources. Perhaps you feel that embracing what you have created, but do not want, is an admission of failure. This fear might be causing you to engage in denial in order to avoid self-recrimination, shame, blame, or guilt. These feelings are very likely causing you to shut down not only to your life, but also to all the potential that exists for you in present time.

Your life and how you feel about it are crystal clear reflections of what is contained in your matrix. If you are unwilling to face what is there, you will never be empowered to change it for the better. In order to examine life honestly, you must learn to separate the facts of your circumstances from the fears and judgments you have about them.

The matrix that is creating your circumstances is your literal agreement with the universe about what your reality will be. When your soul summons resources in an effort to bring about your evolution, it can only operate within the framework of your agreement with the universe. The matrix, therefore, is actually the limit you have placed upon what resources can be brought to you at any given time. The soul's unlimited potential is constrained by your matrix, and only those things that match your agreement will pass through the matrix and be created in your life. That which is actualized by your matrix is only a fraction of what is possible for you. But because the matrix has limited your potential for many years, Mind has probably convinced you that this limitation is fixed and that you are not likely to have a life that is much better than it already is.

If you believe this, it would be a very wise thing to take that belief to the void and invite it to be released!

When energy is converted to form, a creation-event occurs. When you create unconsciously, from the foundation of illusion, the soul summons whatever energy it can devise that fits your matrix. The matrix shapes the energy into experience by a process we call *informing matter*. When matter is informed, it receives its instructions for materialization and generates its form by purposeful intent to carry out its instructions. The result is that you as body and personality have an experience. With each experience, you have the free will to interpret that experience any way you choose. If you choose to cycle it through your old fear-based thought pattern, it will reinforce your matrix by adding substance to the established matching thought-form.

If, however, you consciously withhold your fears and judgments, you instead restore yourself to present time and the field of all possibility where a potential beyond the limits of your matrix can be actualized. Whenever you are able to do this, your awareness expands, and your agreement with the universe is thereby altered by your new perception of reality.

If you are to change your agreement pro-actively, you must examine the nature of the matrix in present time. The way to do that is to examine your circumstances, carefully separating the facts from the way you feel about them. When you do this, it will soon become apparent that you have far more fears and judgments than you have facts. It is easy to see that your thinking is heavily weighted in favor of fears and judgments, and that the facts of your life—few by comparison—are virtually buried under a mountain of emotional reactions generated by Mind.

Your task is to expose Mind, to speak to it directly by acknowledging exactly what the fear is and confronting it. The key to shifting your matrix is learning to be with the immediate truth that confronts you and work with it by bringing yourself into the moment, rather than allowing fear to extrapolate and produce from it more fears and judgments based on illusion.

When you elevate your consciousness to the level of your soul, you become aware of the unlimited resources and help that are available to you in the higher dimensions. You are able to view your life with objectivity, seeing the facts as real and the fears and judgments as illusions of Mind. These thought-forms—your fears and judgments—can then be invited into the void and released to their higher evolution, and that part of the matrix represented by them can be deconstructed and rebuilt from the soul's desires.

The following meditation is designed to assist you in examining your life from the perspective of your soul. This meditation will also allow you to see your life in the context of resonance. It will give you the opportunity to make a clear choice to transform an area that clearly does not resonate or reflect who you are as Spirit. It will take you on a journey through the dimensional layers that are closest to your physical form. We use the word *closest* metaphorically because in reality no dimension is closer than any other dimension. But for the purpose of explaining how creation-events occur, we use the concept of layers because it infers the immediate access you have to the dimensions that impact the reality you create. It also allows you to think in terms of the sequence of steps energy takes during its transformation into a creation-event. When you are finished it may help you see or sense that you are a multidimensional being whose energy exists in many dimensions other than the Earth plane.

Meditation for Examining Your Life

Take a deep breath and enter the void. Invite all limiting thoughts and feelings into the void to be released to their higher evolution. Place your attention on the center of your body, and see or sense your physical body as energy. Move your awareness out to the dimension where you can see or sense yourself as energy in the dimension of your purpose for having a human experience. And moving out another dimensional layer, see or sense yourself as Spirit informing matter. As you move out another layer, see or sense the matrix of your thought-forms as your agreement with the universe about what your reality will be. Any struggle that you have been experiencing and any blocks that you have are residing in this matrix. Recognize that you have the ability through free will to change your agreement at any time you choose. Now, move out yet another layer, and see or sense the dimension where your soul summons resources for your life, growth, and evolution. Pay particular attention to how dynamic and open this layer is, that it is expansive and constantly in motion. As you elevate your consciousness to the next layer, you will become aware of all of the help that is available to you in the higher dimensions. From this elevated perspective examine your life. Find the area of your life that truly resonates with you as Spirit. Then, by contrast, find the area that is least resonant. View this area from the perspective of your soul. Separate the facts of circumstances from the fears and judgments you have about those facts.

Use this meditation any time you feel bogged down or blocked. Notice that much of the charge you have on an issue falls away as you elevate your consciousness. You may also realize that, when you view your circumstances from the perspective of resonance, you can feel more neutral about the circumstances instead of plunging into a spiral of negative emotions. These negative emotions are the judgments and fears that are triggered in Mind by the facts of your circumstances. Begin to notice how Mind obsesses over any fact that does not match up to its expectation. It ruminates on what this fact might imply about the future. It launches into negative evaluations of the way things appear and what they seem to predict about what will happen.

Exercise for Identifying Judgments & Fears About Your Circumstances

Choose the area of your life that is least resonant with your soul. Take a sheet of paper. On one side, list a circumstance—just the facts of that circumstance—and on the other side, list every judgment and fear you have about the fact. Repeat the process, recording a single circumstance on the left and listing all of the fears and judgments you have about that circumstance on the right. Try to identify all the circumstances, fears, and judgments associated with the area of your life that is least resonant.

If you examine this worksheet, the first thing you will notice is that there are far fewer facts than there are judgments and fears. This tells you immediately that Mind has power over you largely because your thoughts, by habit, are so heavily weighted in favor of fear and judgment. If you were to have a window into the fear and judgment list of most people, you would discover that their lists are very similar to yours, even though the facts of their circumstances may be quite different. You would clearly see that Mind's product, fear and judgment, is shared by most of the population.

The other thing you might notice is how much this kind of thinking has affected the way you view your life. There is an opportunity for you to simply change your mind about the circumstances, and this change of mind or heart alone could dramatically improve the quality of your life, simply by removing a fear or a judgment you have.

What you need to understand is the unconscious impact your fears and judgments have on the way your life actually works. You may not be aware how much they act to remove from your awareness opportunities and information that would make your life more joyful. You have seen examples of deeply negative persons and how their anger and bitterness blinds them to any good thing that may exist in their lives. It is so obvious that if these people would release their fear and judgment, the good that is already there would become immediately apparent to them. The same is true of your own life, hopefully to a lesser extent. If you learn to conquer fear and release your judgments, this alone could make you a much happier and contented person, even if nothing in your circumstances were to change.

Meditation for Releasing Judgment & Fear

Take a deep breath and enter the void. Take the fears and judgments from your worksheet and invite them, one at a time, into the void to be released to their higher evolution. Then spend 5 minutes working on the area of the matrix that governs this area of your life. Remember that this process is like an archeological excavation, working layer-by-layer to uncover and release the energy. (This may take several weeks or months if you are working on a deeply held belief, fear, or judgment.)

Many things you hold true out of fear are making your life seem much worse than it actually is. Fears and judgments that are long-held become deeply rooted in the psyche, and they begin to replace the facts of your circumstances with the manufactured reality of the Mind. The fearful scenarios painted by Mind become as real as actual events, and the body and the psyche undergo the stresses of these imaginings as if they had actually happened. As these imagination-induced stress events repeat themselves, the Mind causes you to pull back from life. You do this out of fear and a desire to avoid the suffering that these stress events are creating. It is a vicious cycle that ultimately causes you to retreat into your increasingly negative imagination. The end result is that you invest your life force in trying to avoid or control the outcome of events, rather than creating your life by design from the desires that lay dormant in your heart.

How you think—your matrix in action—acts like a magnet attracting to you what matches up to your deeply held thought-forms. And like a magnet, it also has the power to repel. Your matrix attracts and repels events, people, and things to or from your life. For this reason it is imperative that you undergo routine examination of what your life implies about your matrix. Then you must set about shifting any energy that does not reflect the highest expression of who you are. The more of these judgments and fears that you can release from your matrix, the more awareness you will have of the infinite possibilities that are provided to you by the Creator when you are in present time.

The Essence & Form of What You Desire

You no doubt have a wish list of what you would like to create. This list probably includes objects, experiences, and circumstances, even relationships. Some things you might think of as necessities, others as luxuries. You may also have noticed that the list changes dramatically over time. There may be a few things on your list that were there ten years ago, but most of what you want undergoes a shift as you mature and your circumstances change. What you may not be aware of is this: each of the items on your list has value to you, and you want that item because you expect to feel a certain way if you receive it. And if receiving the item does not produce the feelings you were expecting, the item proves to be very disappointing. It can also make you needy for more as you seek an antidote for your disappointment.

The feeling experience that you hope to have is what we call the *essence*. The item itself is called the *form*.

Mind is always focusing on form. It seeks some forms to fulfill its legitimate needs for power, safety, and value. But most of the forms Mind seeks come from neediness based on the illusion of what Mind fears, and as antidotes for fear, acquiring them becomes addictive. The reason is this: what Mind wants out of fear is never satisfying because it has no essence. This is never truer than when Mind focuses on money.

Money is a form. In your heart you already know that money does not really solve anything on a spiritual level. If it did, everyone you know who had more money than you do would be fortunate enough to have fewer problems and more of the spiritual qualities you have come to respect, like compassion, generosity of spirit, kindness, and so forth. This is clearly not the case. In fact, you might not realize that those who hunger for money because they have none are just as greedy as those who stockpile money to make themselves feel more secure and better able to control what happens to them. This is why it is said that the love of money is the root of all evil. You will notice that money itself is neither the problem nor the solution. What is the problem? It is *fear of the future* imagined by

Mind. How do we solve the problem? We focus our attention on the essence, the feeling experience we want to have. Many of you who think you want money are really after the freedom and fun you hope to have by receiving more of it.

Most of you have learned to think of feelings as a byproduct of having things. But the reverse is true. It is a desire for certain feeling experiences that drives your efforts to have something you think you want. The part of you that is having a human experience is here to undergo the way it feels to be a human being. When you identify the feeling experience you hope to have when you create something, it becomes rather easy to evaluate whether or not you are seeking essence—a desire of the soul—or seeking instead to feed your ego and quell your fears.

The focus on essence is one of the most transforming shifts that you can make in your thinking. When you focus on form, what you are really doing is trying to control the outcome. You close the doors on the Creator's spontaneity, and you do not leave room for Spirit to co-create with you. When you focus on the essence of what you want to create, you open up limitless possibilities by allowing Spirit to bring you that essence in forms you may never have imagined. If you want to change what you are creating in your life, then you must cleave to the truth that life is a feeling experience, and the essence of what you want to create should be foremost in your thoughts.

Exercise for Identifying the Essence of What You Want to Create

Pick something you think you want, an object that you would like to have. Explore the list of essence words in the appendix and see if you can identify what the essence of your desire is. Feel free to pick a word of your own that does not appear the list.

Examine for a moment what would make this object useful to you. Would it make your life more comfortable? Would it save time that you could reinvest in doing something you enjoy? Would it better support your work? Would it more fully express who you are? Conversely, do you want this object solely because you believe it would serve to enhance your prestige, perhaps by making you feel less insecure? Would it make you feel more glamorous and quell your fears about how others perceive you? Would it increase your power over others and thereby compensate for your low self-esteem?

If your desires come from your neediness and fear, they will not have essence. In fact, identifying essence is an excellent tool for determining the orientation of a desire. If you focus solely on form, you may never discover your true reason for wanting something. You may not have the opportunity to examine whether or not the thing you want will satisfy your desire. And worse, you might go to a great deal of effort and struggle to receive the form, only to discover that essence is not there and that you are dissatisfied with the result of all your hard work.

Form is very limiting. It can only be satisfied by strict criteria that match up to it. Essence is expansive. There are limitless ways in which essence can be experienced. And more importantly, the more you attention essence, the more of it you will have. Essence can be experienced in small ways and large ones. For example, the essence of beauty can be felt by simply observing a bird, a flower, or a butterfly in your back yard or neighborhood. The essence of serenity can be found in the breath and using it to bring you into present time. The essence of financial freedom can surely be felt if you win the lottery, but it can also be felt in getting a real bargain, or in the awareness that you no longer need to own, support, and maintain much of the material possessions that clutter your life.

Many of you have asked us how to find love. But when we ask you what it is you want in a partner, you will often give us a list of attributes concerning appearance, income, profession, personal interests, a desire to have children, and so on. It might surprise you to learn that most people who are asked to define what they want in a partner never mention the most important essence of any relationship: *unconditional love*. This is just one example of how a focus on form can mislead you to create exactly what your desired form is, but leave you missing the most important element of any creation: essence.

If you want an easy chair and you are focused solely on form, you might pick something based purely on the way it looked. When you get the chair home, it might only then occur to you that part of what you wanted was a comfortable place to sit and relax with your evening cup of tea. You might discover that while the chair is exquisitely beautiful and matches your color scheme perfectly, it is not a very comfortable chair, and you cannot relax when you are trying to drink your tea for fear it might ruin the delicate fabric should you spill a drop.

Suppose you wanted an easy chair but were afraid that you could not afford one. Or you had a judgment that what you wanted simply was not out there to be found. Perhaps thinking about this made you angry with yourself that you did not make enough income to support your taste and style. And you did not even notice that this kind of thinking is habitual. Chances are you would be so convinced that you cannot have what you want that you would not even get up out of your old chair to seek out opportunities for a new one. You might stay put in an effort to avoid feeling disappointed and angry with yourself. The opportunity for the ideal chair might be as close as your neighbor's garage sale, but you would not notice because your desire had been swallowed up by your judgments.

When you want something, what you desire is a feeling experience you hope to have. If you are needy, you might want security. If you are driven by ego, you may want superiority or domination. In either case what you are after is control. Control takes many forms, some obvious and some subtle. If you feel threatened by someone, and the threat posed makes you fearful, you might want to dominate that person by creating superior strength or weapons. You might want to create a conflict that you could win so that the threat could be eliminated. You might spend a great deal of resources and energy enhancing your ability to win conflicts, and set about creating more of them to enhance your confidence in the superiority of your strength. And when new threats continued to appear, you might feel frustrated, but it might also validate your original fear-based assumptions, because no matter what you do, threats keep appearing.

If you were to approach this problem from the perspective of essence, the first thing you would notice is that the need to dominate out of fear of the future has nothing to do with Spirit. If you were to elevate your consciousness, you might begin to see that the essence of what you want to create is actually serenity and peace. If you focused on these essences, you might discover limitless possibilities for creating harmony, cooperation, empathy, and compassion that might lead to learning more about the issues that led to this person posing the threat. You might seek to understand the underlying conditions that were causing the problem and then resolve the causes rather than react to the behavior. Or perhaps you would realize that this person's problem has everything to do with his own unresolved issues and nothing to do with you. You might then find peace by letting the incident go and moving on.

Essence clarifies for you what it is you want in your heart. When you identify essence in the exercises that follow, you will notice that certain essence words keep coming up. These are the essences that are the most powerful for you because they are the language of your soul. The Mind speaks to you in urges, appetites, and attachments. The soul speaks in desires of the heart. Once you know which essences are most important to you, you can look at your life as it already is and find that you are already receiving a lot of essence.

Essence does not require anything of you. Nothing has to happen. No one else has to do anything. Because essence is the desire of Spirit, it will take you to a place that Mind cannot go. Essence is what your soul wants to experience. When you seek essence and create from the desire to have it, you invite the Creator into the process and ask that divine spontaneity assist you in birthing essence into form.

Many of you wonder why it is that you have asked and asked for what you want, but it seems as if the universe is not listening. The irony is this: you are the one who is doing the creating. When what you have created is not what you want, then your matrix, your judgments and fears, and your focus on form are the real culprits. If you think the Creator is withholding from you, you may want to examine your beliefs by asking yourself: do you believe the Creator is a punishing god who turns a deaf ear to your prayers?

Your matrix is your agreement with the universe about what your reality will be. When your matrix speaks to the universe through the fear-based thought-forms it contains, Spirit will reflect that back to you by sending you an event or circumstance that mirrors whatever negative belief you hold. Does this mean you must be perfectly healed in order to create for yourself? No, on the contrary, it simply means that you must learn to communicate in a way that allows the universe to recognize you as a soul, in present time, expressing a desire for essence.

Detachment from form is vital to the process of co-creation. When you are attached to form, you want specific things to come to you in a certain way, on a set schedule. When this expectation is not met, you assume the worst. Mind goes to work on your confidence, undermining you by telling you that this is proof that you cannot have what you want. It pulls you out of the present moment and blocks your access to the field of all possibility. And in so doing, it actually reinforces your belief that the form is what you want, otherwise doing without it would not disappoint you so much. When you insist upon having the form be a certain way, you have declined the opportunity to dance with the Creator. You have chosen control instead of co-creation. You may be able to create from a need to control; people create this way all the time. But it will be an effort and a struggle, and the universe will not uphold you.

The universe does not assist you in creating from the half-truths of form or the illusion of control. Essence is the absolute truth about what your soul wants from this human experience. When you focus on essence, you reclaim dominion over Mind and transcend the matrix of your thought-forms, thereby transforming it. When you live the expression of essence, fear can be your ally. You can even make fear a partner in the co-creation process because, when you feel it, fear can serve to remind you that you are not in present time and that you are not in touch with what your soul desires.

Meditation for Transmuting Fear into Desire

Take a few breaths to return yourself to the moment. Bring a fear into your aware-ness. Focus your attention on the way this fear affects you physically, perhaps notic-ing what is tense or uncomfortable in your body. Now focus on the essence of what you desire in place of that fear: joy, creativity, ease, freedom, fun, and uncondi-tional love, just to name a few essences. State your desire for the essences that you desire most. Notice the shift in the way your physical body responds to the statement of your heart's desire.

The reason your body relaxes is that a desire for essence is the most authentic thought you can hold. It is a perfect representation of what your soul holds in its heart center. This authenticity is the vehicle by which you conquer fear and bring yourself into the moment, returning your attention to the field of all possibility. The heart is the seat of your courage. When you are speaking from the heart, fear has no place. No one can tell you that you do not desire what your heart wants, and when you speak from heart's desire, you have spoken the ultimate, irrefutable truth of the soul's desire for essence.

The potential for co-creating with Spirit occurs when you are in the present moment. Here, you enter the field of all possibility. You withhold fear and judg-ment and wait until the potential for essence becomes obvious to you. And because you are looking for essence, the form that Spirit brings you might be very surprising.

When you know that a form you have already created is giving you essence, you can then acknowledge that essence. When you acknowledge the essence you already have, you are *living* your dream and turning your desire for essence into reality.

When you desperately want something but cannot identify the essence with any degree of certainty, then it is time to re-examine that desire. You may dis-cover that part of your desire comes from fear, insecurity, or a need to control the outcome. When you find Mind's influence, invite what you find into the void to be released to its higher evolution. Invite that area of your matrix to deconstruct and be released, and create new thought-forms from your soul's desire for joy, creativity, and ease. Ask the Ascended Masters to enlighten your Mind's need for power, safety, and value so that Mind can be restored to its rightful place as your ally.

Exercise for Seeing Essence You Already Have

List six of your favorite essence words. For each essence, identify forms in your life that currently give you this essence. Notice how much essence you already have. Notice that what you feel about your life can change just by acknowledging the essence you have already created. Just for fun, take those same essence words and see how many forms you can think of that would create more of that essence in your life.

A desire of the soul is not a want sandwiched between two judgments. If you notice that you are trying to create this way, you must release judgments in order to expand your awareness of the field of all possibility. Desire is not a want limited by fear of letting go of what is there, or by fear that you cannot create what you want. If you shy away from essence, it may be that you think it will not be enough. Mind may have convinced you that essence is a byproduct of form and that form is the most important thing. The reverse is true: form that satisfies is always a byproduct of essence.

When people ask you what you want, and you do not give them a list of forms, they may tell you that you do not know what you want. If you give them a list of your most treasured essences, they may even tell you that you are confused. Choose not to accept their reality. Recognize that your lack of focus on form is actually a very high state because it means you are hearing only the language of your soul. Realize that if all you know is the essence of what you want to create, you are completely open to the field of all possibility and the spontaneity the Creator has in store for you.

Spontaneity is what the Creator wants to bring to interactions with you. Spirit wants to be creative, joyful and playful, and work without attachment to a plan. What the Creator has in mind is really simple: to dance! When you dance with the Creator, you realize that life as it should be lived is a beautiful dance of joy where both you and the Creator can be spontaneous, open, and imaginative as you co-create in the field of all possibility.

Use of will to push fear away only strengthens it. When you push fear away, you grant it powers that it does not naturally possess. You give it power over your happiness. You give it power over your creativity. You give it power over your freedom. The reason fear has power is that you do not face it. If you confront it face-to-face, you will discover that fear is based on a very weak and pathetic illusion.

Essence *transforms* fear. What you desire as essence is part of who you are. It is the most authentic thought you can hold. State your desire, and it is this authenticity that will assist you in conquering fear. You do not have to believe in yourself to state your desire for essence. You do not have to believe that you can have essence to know that you desire it more than anything. Whether or not you have confidence in yourself, the statement of desire for essence is the truth of Spirit. When you speak it, your request for essence reverberates throughout the higher dimensions. When you let fear remind you to speak your desire for essence, fear becomes your greatest ally in co-creating with Spirit.

Can you be successful without goals and plans?

When Spotted Eagle speaks about living life spontaneously, he certainly understands the need for certain types of planning. Appointments and other structures like budgets and business plans are necessary to any functioning company, but Spotted Eagle believes that they are most useful as statements of our dreams and intentions. And when the universe hands you something that is not in the plan, it is important that you are flexible and detached, focusing on the essence.

Goals and objectives run the corporate world. Employers will often demand that you set and keep goals. What should you do? By all means set and try to keep them, but recognize them for what they are and do not be fooled. Then set about creating with essence. If what you create is not in line with expectations, and attempting to live up to these is making you miserable, then ask yourself if the job you are in provides you with essence. If not, perhaps it is time to create something more in line with your soul's desires.

Goals and objectives measure performance against form. Essence is a measure of being. Financial freedom is an essence that satisfies more deeply and consistently than any goal or plan could ever do. If you had it, would you consider yourself successful?

Actualizing the Possibilities

When you enter the void—the field of all possibility—you open your awareness to all the potential that exists for you in the eternal present moment. Some of this potential is what you would consider negative, and it is the negative potential that is of interest to Mind. The neutral or positive potential may not be as obvious. If you can remain in present time, your awareness of possibilities expands. If you can maintain your expanding awareness of infinite potential, eventually you will become aware of a specific possibility that feels right, do-able, and resonant. What will identify that possibility is essence, and it will probably resonate to such a degree that you will feel no hesitation to act upon it.

When you make a decision or have a judgment or fear, you collapse the field of all possibility into that single actuality. Whatever you perceive is true for you, and no other possibility exists for you beyond it. If you are to remain in the field of all possibility, expanding your awareness of the unlimited potential for what will be, you must root out fear and judgment, and invite them into the void.

Exercise for Describing the Life of Your Dreams

Examine the area of your life that is least resonant with your soul. If you could transform this area into anything that you wanted, what would that be? What is your dream for yourself in this area? It is important when doing this exercise to allow yourself to think beyond limitation. Think as if you were speaking your wishes to a genie who could grant you anything you desired. When you have finished describing your dream, list all the fears and judgments you have and the reasons you believe you cannot have it come true.

Examine the list of fears and judgments you have about what is possible for you. Compare it to the list you made when you were identifying the judgments and fears you have about your current circumstances. You will probably notice many similarities. If you enter the field of all possibility with all of this baggage, what do you suppose will happen?

If you are an extremely fearful or judgmental person, you may be collapsing the field so quickly that your awareness of the possibilities open to you will be very restricted. If you are able to withhold judgment and release fear, you place your attention on the field. As your awareness of possibility expands, you will begin to notice options you were not aware of when you entered the field. It is simply a matter of time before a real and tangible possibility, one that matches your essence, becomes obvious to you. When this happens, you can choose to collapse the field by making a decision to believe in that possibility and then acting on that decision.

If you notice that a fear or a judgment is collapsing your awareness of the field of all possibility, it is your job to immediately take that fear or judgment to the void and invite it to be released. Do not wait to do it at a more convenient time. The process of releasing fear and judgment can be done anywhere, in as much time as it requires to take in a breath and then exhale it. It is important that you develop a habit of releasing judgments and fears as they arise in order to keep them from collapsing the field and adding more substance to your matrix.

Attachment to form increases judgment and fear. If you have attachment to a form, fear and judgment are probably at the root of your attachment. If you were focused on essence, you would realize that you could get the experience of essence from a wide variety of forms. But if you fixate on a certain form, only that particular form will do. The thought of losing it might launch you into fear-based thinking about what might happen in your future were you to be without this form.

Jobs are a perfect example of how attachment to form really works. Suppose you own a home and a car, and the income from your job is what you are presently using to pay the loans you have taken out to purchase these things. If you lose your job, Mind will almost certainly latch onto the potential for loss of these items. If the economy is poor, Mind might stir up fear that another job may not be available to you. You may have a lot of judgments about your ability to take care of yourself. You may have fears about running out of money.

If you decide that the loss of your home and car is the end of the world, you collapse the field of all possibility. Your fears might begin to build. You may become frantic in your attempt to find a way to hang onto these attachments. Foremost in your mind might be the question: *what will happen to me if I lose my house and car?* The very question may terrify you. You might arrive at your first interview, fearful, needy and desperate, so you may not make a good impression to your prospective employer. Or worse, the job may be totally wrong for you—it has no essence—but you might take it anyway out of fear and attachment to your possessions, your present way of life, and your neediness for security. You might tell yourself that this may be the only possibility, so you had better take the job in case no other job is offered to you.

You may not see that there are a host of other opportunities waiting for you if you will only give up your attachment. There may be opportunities for you in a different community. There may be the potential of creating your own business. There may be the possibility of going into partnership with someone whose skills and abilities have excellent synergy with your own. There may be the chance to change your career into something that you really love to do. You may realize that you spend so much time working to pay the loan payments that you hardly spend any time in that house or car, and that your meager enjoyment of these things is not worth the price.

Sometimes giving up attachment means giving up the thing to which you are attached. But more often than not, all you are giving up is your neediness to have things turn out a certain way because you are afraid. If you have an attachment, enter the void and invite that attachment to be released.

If you are having trouble creating what you want, it is important to identify attachment or a fixed idea you may have about the form. Take a deep breath and enter the moment. Realize that there is something else that gives you essence, and that this potential is in the field of all possibility, waiting for you to discover it. If you can maintain the thought that something else is out there waiting to be discovered, your energy becomes open and more dynamic. Your focus on essence in the present moment will draw you to the appropriate form at the right time.

Embracing uncertainty without fear is key to living in the moment. Sometimes your neediness for things to be predictable can cause you to decide something is true, just to have the illusionary certainty of knowing the answer. Some of you are very good at interpreting the matrix. You may travel along it, predicting with a high degree of accuracy what it will produce. But when you reach the point where the matrix is unformed—where its predictability merges with uncertainty—Mind takes that uncertainty and converts it to fear. In this way, Mind capitalizes on predictive thinking and makes you resistant to living in present time.

Almost anything you think about the future is an illusion. The matrix is fluid and can change dramatically every time you change your thinking, so it is not always an accurate predictor of what will be. If you focus on essence, it will allow you to be more comfortable not knowing what form the future will take. In order to truly live in the moment, you must learn to trust that Spirit will bring you forms that are deeply fulfilling because they give you the desired essence. Train yourself to be comfortable with not having the answer. Your power and creativity come from living in the question. Realize that any answer about what will happen in the future is like anesthesia, a drug to bring you relief from your own fear. It is numbing, deadening your feelings and suppressing your natural curiosity. The question—the inquiry into limitless possibility—makes you feel alive. It brings excitement and a sense of adventure into your life. Living in a state of inquiry keeps you from collapsing the field of all possibility into an actuality that you do not want. Further, if something unpleasant happens, the displeasure can be felt in present time and pass quickly into the oblivion of the past. This can only happen when you withhold judgment and fear about the unpleasantness so that you can be present for the next creation-event the universe has in store for you.

Purpose & Intention

You live in a culture that may cause you to believe that you are not whole and complete. It bombards you with fabricated images of beauty and power, and tells you that if you do not live up to these artificial standards, you will not be able to compete effectively for a limited pool of resources, such as money, love, jobs, and the like. The culture's standards may serve to convince you that there is something missing, that you are defective and must compensate for your defects by becoming something other than who you are.

This paradigm of neediness compels you to do whatever it takes, even if you hate what you do, so that you can overcome your inadequacies. The paradigm insists that you do this by acquiring some sort of material power. This power can take the form of wealth, a certain type of physical beauty or prowess, or dominance by force over others or the environment. It can also take the more common form of perceived security. The paradigm of neediness causes you to believe that when you acquire this power, you will become invulnerable to feeling insecure.

It is not difficult to see the suffering that is created by operating within this paradigm. How much of your life have you spent doing something you dislike, or even hate, in order to have something you believe will make you more wealthy, attractive, or secure? Did it work? Did it take away your fear? Probably not, or if it did, this was only temporary. The reason is you were seeking to become something you are not instead of seeking the essence of what you desire most in your heart.

Neediness occurs as a direct result of Mind's prophesies that there is a future out there that is fraught with dangers, obstacles, and lack. Mind tells you that you are inadequate to the task of simply living your life, that you are not good enough, and that you lack the power to meet life where it is lived, in the present moment. Mind convinces you that what you really need is to be something more than what you are. It tells you that you must take action to have those things that will ensure you become what it believes you need to be. It tells you that if you become what you need to be, you will have control over events and therefore feel less afraid. This is how the Mind, through neediness, creates attachment to a certain outcome. It makes that specific outcome or form seem like it is the only thing that will fill this need. Both the need and the form in this case are based on illusion.

There is a paradigm of Spirit. It instructs you to be your authentic self, do what your gifts inspire, and receive essence. In the paradigm of Spirit, doing what your natural gifts inspire is an outflow of being your authentic self. What results from this is an abundance of forms that resonate with you and bring you essence! This paradigm of Spirit is the basis of all higher purpose.

Everything in Creation has a reason for being. This reason for being defines the function of each form in the universe, from an atom to a galaxy. It gives context to all that has been created in the universe. When Spirit informs matter or energy and directs it to take a certain form, it does so by defining purpose. In fact, purpose is a dimension of all being in the universe.

When you create an object, you do much the same. Before you take materials and shape them to your specifications, you have created a purpose that defines what the object will be, what function it will perform, and what it will give you as a result. If you are baking a cake, you assemble things that you would not eat as you find them—like flour, raw eggs, or baking powder—but what you create from them is something that, when baked, is food that has the capacity to give you both sustenance and pleasure. If you are creating a work of art, the same is true. You make an object from a lump of clay, and when you are finished, it is a sculpture that can serve as an object of beauty. That same lump of clay might be formed quite differently if the essence you intend is a sturdy mixing bowl.

When you create your life, your lump of clay is the unlimited potential in the field of all possibility.

As you awaken spiritually, you may become aware that your life as you are living it lacks a sense of meaning. You may want to bring Spirit more fully into your daily activities, but have no idea how this might be accomplished. You may even ask yourself, *why am I here?* The answer is really quite simple. You are here to overcome fear and fulfill your life purpose.

Exercise for Life Purpose, Part 1

On a sheet of paper, make a list of the qualities you like most about yourself. These may be attributes, like compassion, spontaneity, courage, patience, enthusiasm, ingenuity, or perseverance. Invest some time in making this list as complete as you can.

Now, list your natural gifts and talents. You may have a gift with children or animals. You may be a wonderful speaker or a good listener, or excel at organizing tasks and people. You may have a talent for design or engineering. You may be quite skilled at teaching or coaching. You may have powerful intuition or psychic gifts. You may have a gift for making people feel comfortable in awkward situations. List these gifts and talents, as many as you can think of.

Then take a moment to list all of the things you love to do. This list might include travel, sports, cooking, sewing, carpentry, or art. It may include helping people, problem solving, or learning new things. You might love to read books for pleasure or knowledge, to explore ideas and new philosophies. You might love to dance, play soccer, or just sit and do nothing! Whatever it is, do not judge it as trivial, unimportant, or too grand. If you honestly love to do it, write it down!

Now, go back and take a look at the essence words in the Appendix, and select from the list those essences that are most important to you. Feel free to make up your own essence words that clearly express the feeling experience your heart desires. These essence words may include freedom, fun, unconditional love, contribution to others or to the healing of the planet. You may value more than anything independence, truth, or adventure. The list always includes joy, creativity, and ease!

Finally, write down the impact you would like to have on others and in the world. It may be that you want to make the world a more loving or compassionate place. You may want a world where all people understand their creative power. You might desire a world where people and Nature coexist in perfect harmony. Or you may simply want to help those around you to calm down and relax! If you find yourself writing down what you do not want, reframe the statement so that it reflects what you do want instead.

What you have in all of these lists are the ingredients for your life purpose. Your life purpose is your individualized and unique paradigm of Spirit. These ingredients are formed from things that are intrinsic to who you are: your attributes, gifts and talents, things you love to do, and your desires for essence in the world of your dreams. These ingredients require nothing more from you than being who you are already. They are whole and complete and need nothing to perfect them. And when you assemble them into your unique paradigm of Spirit, what you discover is a life purpose that reflects your most authentic self.

Exercise for Life Purpose, Part 2

Complete the form below using your favorite or most meaningful words from the lists you have made in the previous exercise:

My purpose is to be: *(list two qualities, gifs and talents that are your favorites)* as I (do): (*list two of your most favorite things you love to do*)

so that I can experience: (*list two of your favorite essence words*)

and assist in the creation of a world where: (*write in the impact you want to have*)

Now, take this rough draft of your life purpose and reword it to flow more smoothly. Add anything that feels left out.

Your life purpose is your personal context for being. It is your soul's reason for living your life here on the planet. It expresses what your soul intends for you as a spiritual being having a human experience. Life purpose is the highest intention a human being can have. It offers an opportunity to align life and desire with Spirit, and to express intention that defines your unique spiritual path.

When you took a human form, you had an intention. That intention is the same for everything created in the universe: the intention to *evolve*. When you are born into the body, free will is your vehicle for choosing the path by which this evolution takes place. Whenever you set out to create something, you have *intention* to create that thing. If ego, fear and neediness are the context for your intention, what you create will not be aligned with your life purpose, and your path of evolution will be rocky and steep. If your life purpose is the context for your intention, your authentic path of Spirit will be open to you. This path is not always effortless, but it is unfailing in its ultimate satisfaction because the path of Spirit reflects perfectly your soul's intention to evolve.

Spirit's intention cannot exist without willingness. Willingness means that you are willing to face your life as it is in present time. It means that you are willing to examine what you create and tell the absolute truth about it.

Willingness is not a measure of progress. It is a measure of sincerity. Willingness is the way you communicate to the Creator that you sincerely want the growth and healing that you seek. When you are willing, you gain an important measure of neutrality about your process. You begin to realize that growing at a fast and furious pace is not necessarily good and that having a setback is not necessarily bad. This gives you the courage to face whatever your life presents to you because you sincerely desire growth and spiritual evolution. Many times the only way you can shift the energy of your matrix is to create a setback or difficulty. It is important to realize that these times are a reflection of Spirit helping you to actualize your intention to heal.

Your soul has made an agreement with the Creator to have a human experience as part of its evolutionary path. It is your free will that defines the route this path will take. This is why it is a mistake to evaluate your spiritual condition based on appearances that are uncomfortable. When you experience difficulty, it is critical that you reframe your thoughts to include this reality: you are facing these issues because you are ready to address them. All healing crises are legitimate, and it is not appropriate to judge some crises as more worthy than others. Even drama manufactured in the Mind is still, at its core, an issue surfacing in an effort to resolve itself.

Sometimes evolution requires great sacrifice, and sometimes it requires pain. If you can hold fast to the truth that all experience is your teacher, you will be able to see that a teacher of Spirit does not victimize you. Instead it offers you an opportunity to reclaim your innocence.

Fear destroys innocence. Fear eats away at all of the qualities of innocence and humility. It leads to suspicion, arrogance and low self-esteem.

True innocence is an openness that does not pre-judge anything. It is also aware, because without awareness it can be blindsided. It is a state of being completely and totally open to whatever experience is before it in the present moment, even if that experience is painful. Innocence lives in the question and does not require the false security of the answer. Innocence is a state of wonder, a desire to explore, to learn new things, and to experience the richness of life. Innocence and humility have innate within them the motivation to do difficult things and to be free and independent. Even your sincerity can be demonstrated by your willingness to undergo a certain amount of discomfort in order to heal and learn.

Willingness is your most effective tool for bringing the intentions of Spirit into being. It must be the context for all of your little intentions, as well as those that express your highest aspirations. You need to be clear that your soul's over-riding intention is to evolve through the expression of your life purpose. If you attempt to create without the context of life purpose, you may forget your soul's intention and work at cross-purposes with it. If you do that, you may miss the opportunity to evolve more easily by opening the door to co-creating with Spirit and inviting the Creator to dance with you.

Vision

When you imagine what your life would be like if you could have it any way you wanted it, you are said to hold a vision. A vision is like a fantasy but with a few very important differences. Visions are not limited by what you believe to be realistic, possible, or practical. Neither is a vision about the future. It is about the desire you hold in your heart right at this very moment, in present time. A vision is composed of elements that may include material objects, experiences, and feelings, but the key to its construction is essence.

Exercise for Describing Vision & Identifying Essence

On a sheet of paper, write your life purpose. Below that, describe your vision for the area of your life that least resonates with you as a soul. Be brave! Think in unlimited ways that tell the absolute truth about what you want if you could have things be exactly the way you wanted them to be. If you are describing a relationship, for example, remember that it is the qualities of a relationship you are describing and not that you want a specific person to be your partner. Your vision may be composed of forms, feelings, and experiences that inspire you to feel your passion to create them. When you are finished, identify the essence you will experience by having this vision come true.

Examine your vision. Is it aligned with your life purpose? When you read your vision, does it inspire you? If not, you may have limited it by what you think is realistic, or you may be trying to mend what is broken instead of dreaming about your heart's desire.

A vision is not a list of forms you do not yet have. It is not a picture of a future you long for. It is a cherished dream for your life right now, a life that is filled with the essences that matter most to you. If you have essence, then you are already living the life of your dreams in present time, and by doing so, you are fueling your desire for even more essence. But it might be that you actually have essence in your life and do not acknowledge it because you are so focused on the forms you do not yet have. You cannot live the life of your dreams if you have forgotten to attention the essence that already fills your life.

The following is a vision that was created by a student of personal magic whose work, life, and community are described in terms of the essence she wants to create:

My joyful state of freedom becomes a fountain of creativity and a still pool of inner peace, because I am joy, peace, and love, and am exuding positive energy. I am contributing peace, love and harmony in my life and the lives of others.

I am contributing because I am letting my light shine. I am compassionate and playful. It is my playful, compassionate self that exudes love, acceptance, and cooperation with a synchrony and synergy that brings peace, love, and harmony to myself, individuals, families, communities, and children.

I am inviting and attracting others into my spiritual community with playfulness, love, and a sense of humor. I am moving forward, and I have found and continue to find more meaning and happiness by simplifying my life and returning to bond with the natural world. I have attracted many like-minded people who like to share, play, and uplift each other. Through our networking, we are empowered to help return our Earth to balance.

As a spiritual, peaceful warrior and healer for children, I am walking in nature's beauty, offering a helping hand and a loving heart to animals, nature, and humans alike to bring harmony and balance to ourselves and our environment. Everything in my spiritual community is done with our hearts and is completely sustainable. The common thread that integrates within my spiritual community is love and acceptance of ourselves and each other.

It is this self-honoring and acceptance that sparks in me divine energy, unlimited potential, and a fully enlightened loving being of integrity and embodiment of truth. The integration of unity and the sense of humor and play allow a free flow of energy for the highest good of all, and I continuously let go of that which no longer serves. I am touched by the sunshine, and everyone I meet is attracted to me, because I am letting my light shine, and have created a safe space for others to do the same.

You can see from this example that a vision is very different from a goal or an objective. It is an ever-evolving dream that is *lived* rather than achieved. Its focus is on essence and the creation of forms that are birthed from a desire for that essence. And because its focus is not on form, there is no attachment to a certain future outcome.

Attachment to the outcome is a construct of Mind. Mind will tell you that it is an outcome you are trying to create, but this could not be further from the truth. When the Mind gives importance to things, it creates attachment to prevent what it fears. Mind, neediness, and your emotional wounds make unimportant things feel like matters of life and death. It is your neediness that makes having things turn out a certain way seem so important.

Attachment is always founded in a fear that a certain outcome will not come to pass. Attachments create strain, and like overworking a muscle, your attachments create constant tension in your body. This can lead to a cycle of tension and relief, where you are tense when you worry and relieved when your fears do not come true.

Detachment leads to a cycle of joyfulness and neutrality. To detach, you must ferret out the fear that is driving your attachment. As soon as you know what that fear is, you can step into the void and invite it to be released. When you are truly in present time, your attachments dissolve and your desire for essence becomes apparent to you. You realize that anything that has been given importance by your neediness does not matter, and you are able to remember the truth: the only thing that really matters to the Creator is that you evolve.

This is sometimes a difficult truth to accept: that we are here to evolve and nothing else matters. When you look upon your creations, like relationships, jobs, possessions, and other things that make up your way of life, Mind may have convinced you that you cannot live without these things. If you give Mind dominion, you may then try to create from a fear of losing these things. Since the fearful Mind cannot know essence, it cannot create a vision, and your dreams become nightmares filled with what you seek to avoid. One of the most common things you seek to avoid is failure.

Failure is only possible when a goal has been set and performance against that goal is measured. Goals do not operate in present time, and they are therefore meaningless in the realm of Spirit. Goals do not allow for your spiritual journey to proceed with the absolute flexibility that being in present time requires. This flexibility is simply the understanding that everything you dream for yourself today could change dramatically by tomorrow. It is also an awareness that many forms which are not your goals could bring you an abundance of essence.

The problem with goals is that you get very attached to making them happen. Your ego gets involved and lends to the process its preoccupation with appearances. It makes you afraid when you think you may be unable to meet the goal. It is at this juncture that you start pursuing the goal instead of your dream. The path of your dreams is your spiritual path. It is the path your soul asks you to take, and it communicates this through the desire for essence. If you pursue a goal out of fear of failing, soon you will have forgotten the path of your dreams in pursuit of that goal.

When you start measuring yourself against the artificial standards imposed by your goal, you begin to feel your fear acutely. This is ironic because failure is only possible when a dream has been converted into a goal. It can only happen when you arrest the evolution of your dream by fixating on a form that Mind tells you is the only form that will do. Once you have a goal, you ignore your vision and instead devote your energy to pursuing the form that Mind demands. You may manage to create the form your goal requires, but because the goal no longer has the essence of your evolved dream, it will leave you exhausted, empty, and needy for something that will deaden your pain.

To have performance anxiety, you must have a goal, expectation, or agenda. Expectations can be for certain outcomes, or they can be in the form of the expectations you have of others. When there is a goal, the Mind can whisper in your ear, telling you that not achieving the goal is a problem. It will tell you that you won't achieve it because you are inadequate or because some force beyond your control stands in your way. If you allow yourself to become attached to a goal, you may become rigid and frightened when the natural process of the universe adds variables that make the goal difficult or impossible to achieve.

It takes great courage to follow a dream, but follow it you must if you are to live a life filled with essence. And even while you move in the direction of your dream, realize most dreams do not remain the same for very long. They evolve in the blink of an eye, and when they do, they often require that you abandon efforts in which you have made a very large investment. The Mind may try to convince you that the investment is more important than the evolved dream, but if you listen to Mind, you will find yourself yoked to struggle to achieve a goal that has no essence. If you look fearlessly back on your life, you will have to admit that every time you clung to a relationship, job, investment, or possession that had no essence, you turned that area of your life into a burden that made you suffer. And if you bore that burden for very long, you began to lose touch with what you wanted in your heart.

Attachment can be tricky to identify at times. Sometimes it can hide itself within a vision, but you can unmask it if you look for certain clues. One example might be that you want to change another person. You may wish your children were closer to you or that they were married to someone to whom you could better relate. You may be in a relationship that is abusive, and you want your current partner will be nicer to you. Or it may be that you want to change the way your boss treats you or change the way your company does things. This is a trick played on you by Mind. It is called *fixing the form*. Fixing the form is not vision. Vision is the dream to which your heart responds with a desire for essence. Wishing that your partner, boss, or company treated you better may be a perfectly legitimate thing to want, but it limits you severely to that particular partner, boss, or company. Vision has no such limitation.

Vision is self-referring. If you are unhappy with your job, relationship, or family members, then what is happening is you are not receiving essence from these things. Does this mean you have to quit your job, break up with your partner, or sever ties with your family? Perhaps, but perhaps not. When you have vision, you concern yourself with defining the difference between the facts of your circumstances and the way you want them to be. The real question is, can this difference be reconciled so that a vision for essence can be manifested? You may have attachment to your current partner or job, and you may be clinging to what you do not want out of fear or a need for security. What you really desire in your heart is essence and the partner or job that gives you that essence.

Vision and purpose are structures that describe the path you intend your energy to follow. It is important to realize that desire is energy, and that purpose and vision help energy flow in a certain direction, even though they cannot precisely control it. For example, if you drop a ball and nothing interferes with its progress, it will probably fall to certain spot at a certain velocity. What you cannot predict might be a gust of wind that blows the ball off course. Another person might unexpectedly reach out and catch the ball before it hits the ground. Free will and human nature are not predictable things, and life is full of surprises that affect outcomes.

Creating with essence is done by devising a structure that helps energy move in the direction of your intention. Water moving through a river bed on its way to the sea moves more or less within the structure of the riverbed, but there are variables that make this movement somewhat unpredictable, such as weather, the movement of objects like large boulders, the construction of dams, or other much smaller changes that happen over time due to erosion.

If you were to set about creating a river, you might have a rough idea where in the geography it will flow and where the water will end up when it has progressed along the course you intend it to follow. But it is also true that whatever the source of your headwaters for this river, the water flowing along the riverbed has no goal to reach the sea. If it gets there, it does so by behaving naturally according to its characteristics as it moves within the structure into which it was released. It is also true that you would not try to create a river that flows to the sea by placing your headwaters in a desert sink.

When we look in Nature, we can see very clearly how energy naturally matures into forms. Seeds germinate and become plants. Blossoms are pollinated

and become fruit. Caterpillars become butterflies. They do this through a structure known as DNA, the essence that informs cellular energy and tells it what
form to take. If there were no DNA, there would be nothing created from the
collection of substances that make up a plant or a butterfly. The structural information in the DNA is what allows the form to coalesce around the essence the
DNA describes. This structure of energy has to be there in order to ensure that
the energy matures to *fruition*.

Fruition is what happens when energy matures within a structure. This structure can be your matrix, or it can be your desire for essence. One of the things
that make creating difficult for people is that they do not set up the structure that
will allow energy to mature the way they intend. Instead, to make their river, they
may go to the middle of the desert and pour their water onto the sand, watching
it evaporate or disappear between the grains. They do not, for whatever reason,
take the care to observe and consider how the energy will mature to fruition.
Those who are successful consider the mountains as their location for their headwaters, knowing that gravity will be one of their tools. They know the kind of
river they want to create and choose the terrain that will be best suited to guiding
the water in the way they intend, either as rapids or a meandering stream.

You cannot control how energy will mature. If there is a lesson that will assist
you in evolving, your soul may bring it to you by placing in the landscape something you did not foresee. When you encounter this spontaneity of Spirit, be flexible and allow energy to follow its natural course to fruition. If you have set an
inflexible goal that the water must run straight to the sea as the crow flies, you
may quickly learn that very few things in Nature proceed on such a straight and
narrow course.

When an artist sits down to create a work of art, she begins with an idea or
concept about what will be created. Inherent in the process are certain variables,
such as the artist's level of skill, the nature of the materials, and the unexpected
ideas that the process itself might stimulate. This is the principle of *uncertainty*.
The trouble with goals is that they do not allow for the universe to co-create with
something unexpected and spontaneous that might redirect the energy away from
the goal. Attachment to the goal prevents this kind of creative spontaneity in the
dance of co-creation.

Spontaneity is the way of the universe. Goals are empty like the shell of a rot-
ten nut. When you pursue this single nut, you lose sight of the fact that the tree
might be full of many other quite wonderful nuts. When you embrace the nut
tree and surrender your goal for the single nut, you see a more holistic picture:
some nuts will mature, and some will wither and drop off. Some will spoil, and

animals and birds will eat others. You know when the season is over you will probably get some nuts, more in some seasons than others. If you spend your days hovering over the tree out of fear, you may produce a few more nuts, but your life will be filled with unnecessary stress, and it is doubtful that you will truly enjoy the harvest when it finally matures. The most you might hope for is to feel relief that your worst fears were not realized.

When you embrace the principle of fruition, you can surrender your attachment to goals because you understand that goals are artificial and meaningless creations of Mind. You realize that it is no more appropriate to celebrate achieving a goal than it is to be upset if you do not achieve it. Instead, you can live in the truth: fruition is a process that allows things to evolve to their natural conclusion. You must learn to dream in such a way that the dream does not become a goal, because a goal does not allow for fruition. When a dream evolves, essence goes with it. If the old dream turns into a goal out of fear or attachment, it will be devoid of essence. The reason is the old dream is no longer your authentic desire, and when something is not authentic, it is so because it no longer has essence for you. The new dream, however, clearly reflects the essence you desire.

If you must have a goal for some external reason, it is critical that you do not become attached to it. If you find yourself worrying that your dream will not come true, examine how you think about it. Have you made your dream into a goal? Have you become attached to having the form of your vision rather than living the essence?

Reframe what you worry about in the context of your vision. Use these insecurities to identify where Mind has taken you. If you feel a great deal of reluctance to move in the direction of your dreams, examine the issue with your heart's courage. Bring the void—the field of all possibility—to you and then move into it. Your vision will serve to gently guide your course in the direction of its fruition.

Being Your Authentic Self

Every human being is born with gifts of Spirit. Some of you have a natural gift for listening and observing. Others of you have a talent for acquiring and using information, still others for helping people discern what is real in situations that are emotionally charged or confusing. Some of you are artistic, intuitive, or articulate. Others of you have a gift for creating relationships or for healing energy in the body. These natural gifts and countless others are all expressions of your authentic self.

When you are using your natural gifts, what you do is much easier than when you struggle with what does not resonate with you. When you are learning something that employs your gifts, you experience less struggle and have innate motivation to learn and grow, even though learning may require an investment of time and energy. But more importantly, using your natural gifts leads you in the direction of creating things for the highest good for yourself, for others, and for the world. The reason is simple: when you are doing what comes naturally, doing is an outflow of being who you are as Spirit. The creation of the life you want is inevitable because you are being your authentic self, living your authentic life, placing your attention on your authentic desires.

Your life purpose instructs you exactly how to be your authentic self, do what your gifts inspire, and receive essence from what you create. Your life purpose describes your soul's intention for your spiritual path. Authenticity, then, is really about living in the truth of your soul's instructions as you move in the direction of your evolving vision for essence.

When your life purpose directs your course, you acknowledge your spiritual power to create forms that bring you the essences you desire most. When you bring purpose and the power of your authenticity together in present time, what you do releases a kind of alchemical energy that flows into the structure defined by your heart's desire for essence, just as the water of the river flows through the riverbed. As the energy matures to fruition, a form that gives you essence is manifested.

This process is obvious when you observe those who are actively engaged in doing what they love to do. Their lives function in an enviable way. Their work does not feel like work to them. They earn money for doing what they would cheerfully do for no compensation at all. They may work long hours and do hard work, but they feel and project a sense of freedom that is palpable. This is because resources that support their work come to them without meticulous planning, sacrifice or struggle. They are in the *flow*.

The flow is an unlimited, unceasing tide of energy, resources, and support that comes to us when we are being our authentic selves and living our authentic lives in the now. Flow is a natural result of the following things:

> *staying in **present time**,*
> *being your **authentic self**, living your **authentic life**,*
> *creating from your **desire for essence**!*

You cannot be your authentic self if you are not in present time. Mind will work tirelessly to make you believe that being who you really are, doing what your gifts inspire, will not create the life you want. It may confuse you into thinking that you are not the whole and complete human being that is your authentic self. This is how Mind uses fear to block authenticity. If you refuse to follow your evolving dream out of fear, you sacrifice your authentic desires, and in so doing deny yourself access to the full potential of the moment, which is the key to living in the flow. If you anchor your consciousness in the moment, Mind cannot deceive you because Spirit has dominion over Mind in present time. In present time, the truth and power of your authenticity are apparent to you, and the alchemy of the moment is fully accessible.

Authenticity is reflected in your thoughts, your feelings, your desires, and your actions. When you are being your most authentic self, what you do moves you in the direction of your dreams, and creates forms that bring you the feeling experience you desire most. These feeling experiences allow you to *live* your dream in an ever-expanding flow that is sourced by Spirit. The flow is Spirit's response to your expression of the truth of who you are and the authenticity you live in present time.

Stalkers and Dreamers

There are qualities of authenticity that define many of the character traits that shape your personality. These qualities have an enormous impact on how you deal with life and the way you express your authenticity. The two qualities are more than just personality styles. They represent how life, relationship and communication are approached and how you process information. The two qualities are *Stalking* and *Dreaming*.

Stalkers are the shakers and the movers of the planet. They are impatient, restless, outspoken and decisive. Dreamers are the holders of visions and dreams for humanity. While they are equally capable, they are generally more patient, quiet and contemplative than Stalkers.

Stalkers *know*. They know the big picture and understand the grand scheme of things, and they have a very clear idea of what they want. Stalkers are very assertive, and if out-of-power, they can have very little respect for the boundaries of others. If they feel victimized, they tend to resort to tactics that are quite controlling and even overbearing. Stalkers like to get things out in the open and cannot stand to leave conflicts unresolved. This can cause them to be relentless in the pursuit of resolution, thereby making matters worse in cases where a little time and distance might resolve the problem more satisfactorily. Stalkers rarely have a good sense of timing because their agenda and schedule are what drive their impulse to act. This can cause them to force things to happen according to schedule when waiting for a better time or more information might be more advantageous.

Often when Stalkers think they are sharing their feelings about a conflict, what they are really doing is trying to control the behavior of their antagonists through guilt. They often mistake their emotional reactions for truth, and when they are emotional, they may have a difficult time understanding the difference between objective fact and their opinions. It is not uncommon for a Stalker to speak out of turn, offer unsolicited advice that is not welcome, or go on and on about a subject that is making everyone around him deeply uncomfortable. Because they tend to approach social gatherings as an opportunity to display their superior intelligence and show off what they know, they may appear to be insensitive know-it-alls. This is unfortunate because Stalkers usually have their hearts in the right place, but they are often not aware of appropriate timing or how much to say. Because they operate from an agenda about what they decide needs to be said, they might miss the cues that could help them understand the effect they are having. They often say too much, not realizing that more is not necessarily better and that others, especially Dreamers, might need to receive the information in more digestible doses. When a Stalker can learn to speak from the heart instead of his intellect, he can show more respect for the boundaries of others. Then his message is more likely to be understood and appreciated for the spirit in which it was intended.

Dreamers *see*. They see their world in the details and subtleties. They often do not know what they want until they see it and can tell if it feels right to them. They are not assertive by nature, but if out-of-power they can have very high levels of aggression. If they feel victimized, they can react with surprising hostility, given their normally passive temperament. Dreamers tend to avoid conflict and will almost always opt for the course that mollifies their detractors. This can cause their relationships to suffer from distancing and a lack of honesty when conflicts are ignored and allowed to magnify. Dreamers are always waiting for the right time to take action, but if they are not in present time, they tend to wait too long to act and sometimes wait until circumstances force them to act. If they are shy, they may be afraid to share anything of themselves socially, and the bland or silly impression they make may be very different from who they really are.

Dreamers need to learn to speak up so that their concerns may be addressed. They often make the mistake of thinking that everyone can read their minds and that what they think and feel should be obvious. If they are out-of-power, they may withhold vital information that would resolve their problems. If they do not feel it is safe to speak, they may then wait until the situation reaches the breaking point before disgorging long withheld complaints and grievances. They need to choose partners who will listen to them; otherwise they will likely become lost in the relationship and never understand how to relate honestly to their partners.

Most Dreamers find inactivity of any kind very soothing if there are no demands placed upon them at the time. Inactivity for a Dreamer is an opportunity to tune into himself and his environment and achieve a kind of meditative state where his thoughts and feelings take on a dream-like quality that he finds very relaxing. Dreamers get a lot of inner work done in their dreams. Their dreams, when they remember them, can be quite vivid and full of information and extraordinary symbolism that, when heeded, can guide them on their path.

But they must take care not to believe in their nightmares; these bad dreams are really only reflections of the fears they need to address.

Stalkers accomplish a great deal by doing many things at once. They are rarely at rest and often deliberately forego sleep in order to pursue more of their agenda. While a Dreamer can relax by doing little or nothing, the Stalker finds inactivity maddening and will always need something to occupy her restlessness, even when she is relaxing.

Because Stalkers are more assertive and have clear ideas about what they want, it would be easy to think that only Stalkers can be leaders, but this is not the case. Dreamers simply lead by different means. For example, the Stalking leader's vision is a list of things he is determined to accomplish through others. His vision is often composed of solutions to problems he knows could be corrected in order to make things function better and more efficiently. He communicates what it is he wants done and how he wants it done. He motivates by rewarding performance. The Dreaming leader holds and communicates a vision that paints a picture of how he would like his world to be. His vision is one he hopes will inspire those under his leadership to pursue his ends. He motivates by learning the dreams of those he leads and showing them how supporting his dream will help them fulfill their own.

When out-of-power, a Stalker can be very dominating and controlling if he feels that something stands between him and what he wants to accomplish, and he will typically push his agenda at any cost. Those under his leadership may withdraw their support as they begin to see him as arrogant and out of touch with reality. He may eventually be forced aside after having antagonized his former supporters.

The out-of-power Dreamer tends to have a vision that is too blurry or self-serving for others to readily share. If he is feeling misunderstood and threatened, he will tend to withdraw into his own little world, leaving those he leads feeling lost and without direction. His behavior often leaves a power-vacuum. The competition for power that ensues may provoke those under his leadership to abandon him and lend their support to his rivals.

When a Stalker makes a decision, she does so based on a rapid assessment of generalities. She is much more comfortable with decisive action and is happy to deal with the consequences later. If at some point she does not like the consequences or feels they are not worth the effort, she will attempt to make a new decision in order to correct the problem. Because the Stalker is more concerned with accomplishing her agenda, she is confident that even though some decisions will not be correct, in the end she will accomplish more by decisive action than by taking greater care. When a commitment goes bad, she will first try to salvage it, but if this proves impossible, she may find a way to extricate herself from it. It is rare to see a Stalker shy away from a conflict, but if she knows she cannot win the fight, she may resort to avoidance while she devises a strategy in which she has more confidence.

When a Dreamer makes a decision, she does so based on analysis of the details. She is very concerned that the decision be the right one. This is because when a Dreamer makes a decision, she will feel compelled to carry out that decision, even at great personal cost. This is why Dreamers hate living with the unintended consequences. Once a Dreamer makes a commitment, she will suffer greatly trying to keep it, so she knows she had better make the right choice. It will not often occur to her to try to change the terms of the commitment because doing so might create a conflict. Because Dreamers take a long time to make up their minds, they often earn a reputation for being indecisive or uncommitted. But actually, the reverse it true: they are so deeply committed that they learn not make commitments lightly. If a Dreamer is out-of-power, he may vacillate between paralysis and impulsive action, each tactic driving him back in the direction of the other in a vicious cycle of nail-biting fear and self-recrimination.

Stalkers tend to be very expressive and intense about their feelings, yet often with little concern for the consequences their outspokenness might bring down upon them. Dreamers tend to keep their feelings to themselves and have difficulty sharing them unless they trust that their feelings will be respected. Stalkers often get a reputation for being insensitive to the feelings of others because they consider feelings to be only one of many things to be equally considered. Dreamers tend to consider first the way something makes them feel and put most other considerations as secondary.

Stalkers tend to thrive under pressure and like having multiple priorities to juggle. They change gears quickly and are very good at multi-tasking. They want things done a certain way and tend to feel thwarted when their directives are not carried out to the letter. Because they do not tend to study the details, they often make demands that seem unreasonable to those who must carry them out. Very often this difficulty comes when the Stalker's agenda is linked to a schedule that has been made without regard for the magnitude or complexity of the task involved. They often have expectations driven by their agenda, and when these expectations are disappointed, they have trouble taking responsibility for having expectations in the first place. A Stalker's perfectionism can get him into trouble when he becomes inflexible and does not listen to input from others who might have a different approach.

A Dreamer's greatest concern is that he be given enough time and resources to get the job done. If he is working under the supervision of another, he usually prefers to have priorities spelled out for him so he does not risk making a mistake that will create a conflict or an unintended consequence. He hates being rushed and resists when he is pressured. If the Dreamer is a perfectionist, he may have trouble finishing things on a set schedule and have difficulty knowing when additional effort will not significantly improve the results. If pressured to do something he does not want to do, however, he will often do an inadequate job in order to discourage further demands.

Stalkers like being in charge, but they are happy to subordinate themselves to any higher authority whose directives make sense to them. They want to be respected for their knowledge, skills, and accomplishments. They hate having their authority questioned and will actively suppress the efforts of anyone who stands between them and their agenda. They are concerned not only about what gets done but also how it gets done, and when threatened, they will often resort to power-struggles and rigidity that stifle creativity and initiative. When their vision is not clear to them, or when they are deeply fearful, they may engage in a flurry of pointless activity just to make themselves feel as if they are really doing something about their problems. If they have no clear vision, they may waste a great deal of effort trying to accomplish something—*anything*—just to avoid feeling like they do not know what it is they want. If the underlying problem is the way they make other people feel, they will have a very difficult time solving it because when they are under pressure, their own feelings are the only ones that feel real to them.

Dreamers like following leaders who value their hopes and dreams. They want their feelings respected. They hate being discounted and will passively sabotage any effort they feel dishonors them. Dreamers are concerned about how things impact their emotions. When threatened, they will often become obstructive, drag their heals, or completely withdraw. Deprived of their dream or deeply fearful, they lose energy, and their productivity grinds to a standstill.

When a Stalker feels that her nature makes her too challenging for others, she may attempt to live her life as a Dreamer in order to be more acceptable. This rarely works because, when under pressure, a Stalker can rarely maintain the Dreamer façade, and her relationships can suffer terribly for it. Her intimates may come to think of her as a *Jekyll-and-Hyde* and begin to shrink from her because they do not know what to expect and feel intimidated by her volatility. One moment she may be kind and nurturing and the next, authoritarian and demanding. Because she puts so much energy into hiding her natural impatience, her frustration with things tends to boil over in what to others might be seen as completely unpredictable fits of temper. She may resort to blame and judgment that ultimately leave her feeling bitter and unappreciated.

When a Dreamer feels that dreaming is not adequate, he may try to emulate the behavior of a Stalker in order to feel more powerful or less vulnerable. This is usually not to his advantage because when he dons the Stalker mask, it robs him of his attention to his own feelings that are really more important to him than anything. Divorced from the sensitivity that is his greatest gift, he loses touch with his authenticity. The result may be that he is constantly presenting an image that he believes will impress those around him, and he may find himself labeled superficial or hypocritical. He may try to act decisively, but since he cannot handle the mistakes that decisiveness ultimately creates, he may wind up feeling victimized by his failures. He may react by obsessing over minutia, unable to discern what is truly important. Eventually, it may cause the Dreamer to become cynical and angry as he continues to try wielding authority that no one respects for very long. This may, in extreme cases, cause him to behave in a manner that is increasingly pompous, aloof, and even belligerent.

Western Culture does not value Dreaming. This leaves most Dreamers feeling inferior and convinces many Stalkers that they are superior. Because there is no cultural support for Dreaming, out-of-power Dreamers may struggle to find their place in the scheme of things. This is probably the most ironic of all situations because the Creator is a Dreamer, and the universal matrix might be considered the Creator's dream.

Age turns most everyone into a Dreamer. Because Western Culture does not value Dreaming, the wisdom that is a part of all great leadership is often missing. But where Dreaming is valued, the elderly who are wise have a place of honor and can lend powerful assistance to the health and well being of the members of their society. When wisdom and experience are valued in a culture, it is the aged Dreamers who are consulted by those who lead. This allows those with wisdom and experience to contribute and serve as a balancing factor against high emotion and impulsiveness.

Dreamers must confront death before they can fully come into their power. Sometimes this confrontation is literal, in the sense of a near-death experience. But more often than not it is symbolic, a confrontation with their deepest fears. A Dreamer's entire life will reflect the need to have this confrontation until he finally is willing to face it. This is because the Dreamer is here to learn how to claim his power over fear and take action on his own behalf.

Stalkers do not fear death half so much as they fear anything that might impair their power. Stalkers possess a great deal of power and the will to use it, so their greatest tests often involve situations where they may be tempted to use their power to manipulate and dominate others. The Stalker's lesson is about abuse of power, and he may spend his entire life learning how not to control out of fear.

The main thing that separates Dreamers from Stalkers is the way they view the Creator and the universe. Dreamers know the Creator because they see in detail the majesty, intricacy, and beauty of Creation. When they look upon Creation, they feel the Creator's presence and sense their relationship to the divine. They are content to know the Creator through the works of Creation and enjoy the experience of looking deeply into what the universe presents. Stalkers know the Creator through understanding what makes the universe tick. Their desire to know the how and why of the universe is insatiable, and they actively pursue knowledge so they can know more deeply how the Creator makes events in the universe happen.

Although Stalkers and Dreamers have very different approaches to life, they have equal power in creating what is important to them. When they participate as equal partners in an endeavor or relationship, their respective differences can be of enormous mutual support and encouragement. Their combined efforts have the potential to create a whole that is much greater than the sum of its parts.

Personal Magic

When you are being your authentic self in present time, the alchemical possibilities available to you are expressions of personal magic. We call these expressions *magic* because invoking their power generates creation-events that actualize your vision and give you essence. Personal magic represents your personal style of creating. It is composed of gifts, talents and traits that reflect the way your soul has chosen to express itself in this lifetime. Each of you chose to be a Stalker or a Dreamer, and you also chose a primary personal magic. These choices provided you with natural gifts that support your soul's intention for your spiritual path. As you matured, you probably developed secondary skills in other magics. In fact, most of you use all of the magics at one time or another. When you can learn to do so *deliberately* and with intention, you will find that areas of your life that were once a creative challenge become more effortless.

Personal magic usually offers solutions to our most pressing problems. In fact, when you are under pressure, you are often being challenged to use your primary personal magic instead of allowing Mind to dominate your reality. When you are under emotional stress, you are probably inclined to do just the opposite of what your magic suggests. This tendency to allow Mind to separate you from your magic is part of the lesson you are here to learn: to anchor yourself in present time and employ your spiritual gifts in the service of your own higher good.

Each individual's experience of reality is unique. This is evident when a number of people observe the same incident but give radically different accounts of what actually happened. It is just as true for children as it is for adults. Personal magic, and the qualities of Stalking and Dreaming, represent a dramatic influence on the way a child processes information and how he interprets what he sees. Where a Stillness Magic child might be highly attuned to abandonment, his Illumination Magic sibling may be more aware of unreasonable rules and restrictions. This is one reason that siblings of different magics who undergo life experience with the same parents may perceive identical events in such a different light.

There are eight personal magics that are common to almost everyone who walks the Earth. They are Time Mastery, Sex Magic, Void Traveling, Stillness

Magic, Phoenix Magic, Illumination Magic, Healing Touch, and Sacred Weaving. Each magic carries with it a power, a purpose, and gifts. As you review the magics, you will probably notice that you possess some degree of skill in almost all of them, but that one of them seems to be more prevalent in the way your conduct your life. You will see that magic is more than abilities and talents. What magic brings is an approach to living that gives you confidence and authority over your own life because it allows you to be and express your authentic self.

Just as Dreamers and Stalkers can hide behind each other's masks, some of you have taken on a magic that is not your own and have attempted to live your life as if this magic were your primary magic. Those who attempt this may develop a great deal of skill in the magic they are emulating, but creating will usually be a struggle because this secondary magic, while useful, has a dramatic impact on their authenticity.

You will notice that each magic has certain challenges and things that it does not do particularly well. These challenges are part of the reason you chose your primary magic. Overcoming these challenges was very likely a large part of the spiritual growth your soul intended for you when making a choice between the magics. When you know what your magic is, you are better equipped to meet these challenges with more neutrality and compassion for yourself.

But there is perhaps a more significant use for magic, and that is to promote greater acceptance and understanding between yourself and another. This is because, once you understand how the magics and qualities influence the personality, you will be able to honor the distinct differences between yourself and another. Understanding personal magic can make you less frustrated with others and help you to truly support them in creating from the power of their *own* authenticity, even if their style of creating is quite different from yours. This is true in close personal relationships, but it is also true in relationships between employers and employees, between business associates, advisors, and clients, and between practitioners and patients.

TIME MASTERY

Power: to observe the field of all possibility

Purpose: to be in the present moment

Gifts: patience, keen powers of observation and timing, ability to identify opportunity

Time Magic people create not from *doing*, but from *being*. In fact, if a Time Master attempts to create by pursuing an opportunity, he will usually fail or find that the effort it takes is more work than it is worth. Time Mastery creates through the principle of serendipity or what appear to be happy accidents. When a Time Master has the confidence to simply *be* and observe, perfectly timed opportunities spring up out of nowhere. If you ask a Time Magic how he created the best things in his life, he will probably shrug his shoulders and tell you he does not know how he did it. This is because he probably did not *do* much of anything. Instead, he no doubt happened to be at the right place at the right time.

He might have been surfing and noticed something that would make a better surfboard. He may have turned this idea into a small business that he sees as a means to doing more surfing, an activity he loves to do more than anything else. He might have found himself at a party where he met a surfboard manufacturer who just happened to be looking for an innovation that would help increase interest in his product line. Even if this invention and his connections make him a wealthy man, the Time Master's success will no doubt feel to him like a coincidence that had very little to do with anything he actually did.

Time Masters are here to master the eternal present moment. While everyone must be in present time to have access to magic, for a Time Master the eternal now is his home, his playground, and his tool for manifesting. When a Time Master enters a state of simply being in present time, he can use his exceptional observation skills and keen sense of timing to identify opportunities and turn them into actualities. When he is worrying or otherwise out of present time, no access to opportunity is available to him, and his creativity comes to a standstill.

Time Magic people often have no sense that they have anything to do with what they create. If a Time Master is out-of-power, she may feel that her life happens to her and that she has no influence over events. Instead of a life filled with happy accidents, her life is a grim collection of unhappy ones. In fact, Time Masters are often deeply marked by tragedy and may have no outlet for their grief. They may have trouble letting go of past pain and wrap themselves in a mantle of suffering caused by reliving past trauma as though it happened only yesterday. Or they may run away from pain by running away from anything that reminds them of it or by withdrawing into a shell. Addictions may also be a vehicle for their retreat.

Time Masters often get a reputation for doing everything at the last minute. What others may view as putting things off is often just a function of the Time Master's very keen sense of timing. Timing plays a crucial role in everything they do, but when they are worrying about the future, they may delay critical action simply because they cannot see timing when they are not in the now. Anyone who has been close to a Time Magic knows that he cannot be rushed and that he must do things in his own time. If forced or pressured, a Time Magic will often sabotage the effort to prevent whoever is pressuring him from doing it again. If compelled to do something that is not right for him, the Time Master will often fail utterly in the task as his only means of defending his right to make his own choices.

Time Magic people are very accepting of the way things are, even if they do not like their circumstances. This can cause conflict in their relationships, especially if they become deeply resigned or apathetic. A partner may get frustrated if she believes her Time Magic mate is not doing anything to solve his problems. If a Time Magic is out-of-power, he may sit and do nothing while his entire life falls apart. But just as often, what is happening is that the Time Magic is observing and waiting for the right opportunity and the right timing.

Time Masters need a lot of downtime. They need time to daydream and often get their most fantastic inspirations when they are sitting in Nature or staring into space. For these reasons, Time Magic is most closely associated with Dreaming because Dreaming and Time Mastery share a focus on the finer details of things. Many of the characteristics of Dreaming are emphasized in a Time Master. His need to simply be tends to resonate more with a Dreamer's passive, contemplative temperament.

Stalking Time Masters have a particularly difficult time integrating their impatient, action-oriented nature with their need to simply be. When out-of-power, the Stalker nature will abuse and punish the Time Magic side, judging it as lazy and unmotivated. It will prompt the Time Magic to ignore her need for rest and recreation, thereby restricting her access to her magic. Integration usually comes when the Stalker side becomes aware that it knows how to wait for what it wants, and that pushing for things usually produces unwanted results. Another area that creates a dilemma for the Stalker is the Time Master's need to accept what is. Stalkers have a very difficult time accepting what is if they do not like it, and they will want to immediately launch into action to change what they do not like. The Time Master must negotiate with his Stalker nature, pointing out that action without observation and timing will, at best, be a waste of time.

If a Time Magic feels blocked, he needs to stop *doing* and get himself into a state of *being*. He needs to sit on a park bench and feed the birds, or watch a sunset, or enjoy a good book just for pleasure. In general, what Time Masters need is just that: *time*. Time to ponder. Time to make a decision. Time to process information and figure things out. Time to decide what is right for them and what is not. They often do not know what they want until it makes its appearance, and they are most comfortable puttering with their hobbies or just sitting around doing nothing. But the truth is, there is more going on than is obvious because what they are doing is *observing*.

There is almost nothing that escapes the attention of a Time Magic who is in the moment. They have an amazing command of the finer details and are often excellent judges of character because they take a long time to observe and evaluate the nuances of behavior. Because they do not ignore or skip over the details, they may become very bogged down in the minutia and have little awareness of the big picture. For this reason, they tend to think tactically and will often get themselves into trouble if they have difficulty thinking ahead. Most Time Masters do not make good strategists, but no one is better than a Time Magic at implementation. Where strategic thinkers make assumptions that may prove to be incorrect, the Time Magic will often be the one who spots a flaw in the assumption. They usually have the ability to sense the emotional energy in a situation long before they understand the mechanics. When pushed to do something before the timing is right, they will stubbornly resist and may refuse to do the thing at all if pushed too far.

A Time Magic's destiny is usually something he stumbles upon unexpectedly. It is almost never something he plans or pursues. Through being, the Time Magic allows his destiny to find him. For this reason it is probably a good thing that he is also gifted with the patience to wait. In fact, patience is a Time Magic's greatest virtue.

When a Time Magic is in his power, he is in the moment and observant. What he is actually doing is monitoring the field of all possibility. Where other magics travel the void to gain information or seek answers, the Time Magic simply observes what is happening in the field, and upon noticing a possibility that is synchronized with his desires, he captures this realization and actualizes it. This makes Time Magic people very creative. Time Magics are also very sensitive. They are often artistic and have great skill as craftspeople, programmers, engineers, and inventors, where their patience, keen observation and attention to detail are utilized to full advantage.

Time Magic is about the mastery of the continuum of what physicists call space-time. Powerful Time Masters have an understanding that time is plastic, that it can be stretched or speeded up. They have the ability to shrink time when they are engaged in something they dislike doing and the ability to make time stretch when they are doing something they love. Time Magic is also about mastery of the dimensions in the universe. A Time Magic has an astonishing ability to travel the dimensions and find the one where a certain energy already exists, like the solution to a problem, or an answer to a dilemma, or a resource she might need.

If you are in a relationship with a Time Master, it is important that you honor his need for privacy, solitude, and rest. If you can see that he is frustrated or blocked, do not try to push him into action. Instead, encourage him to take a break, get out in Nature and do some daydreaming. If the Time Master is your boss, give him time to digest proposals put before him, and be responsive to any concerns he may have about the details of your proposal. If he is your subordinate, give him all of the details involved; then give him time to assimilate your requests and get back to you with his assessment. If things need to be done by a certain time, allow the Time Magic to respond with alternatives if he feels he cannot meet expectations. He might very well see something critical that you have missed.

If the Time Master is your child, allow him to be a late bloomer. Give him a break between high school and college, and realize that college may not be appropriate until he decides what it is he would like to do. Whatever you do, do not push him into something you think is good for him. This will nearly always backfire. Instead, trust that once his opportunities are obvious to him, he will approach any task with enthusiasm and determination, and will work very hard at whatever his chosen field.

Time Magic is an excellent tool for figuring out what options and opportunities are available. Use Time Magic when you feel stuck or limited; it will open you to possibilities that may not be obvious. If you are a Stalker, the use of Time Mastery will help you in situations where you may need patience, acceptance or a better sense of timing. Invoking Time Magic will allow you to stop and observe what is going on so that you can detect the subtle nuances that you might otherwise miss. Of course, there is no better magic to use for creating rest, recreation or camaraderie. It is the perfect magic for use by parents who would like to feel a deeper connection to their child's playful and inquisitive nature.

SEX MAGIC

Power: to attract

Purpose: to be in the creative flow

Gifts: charisma, spontaneity, attraction of opportunity

Sex Magic is the ability to harness the creative power of desire and use it to step into the flow. When a Sex Magic knows what she wants, she usually has great power to simply draw it to her. For this reason, Sex Magic people are often the subject of great envy among their peers. They typically have extraordinary ability to attract desirable sexual partners. Doors appear to open easily for them, both professionally and socially. When they ask for what they want, they usually get it. And because they are so charismatic, everyone wants to have them around.

Even if a Sex Magic is not particularly attractive, his appearance and energy are often so entrancing that it is difficult to take your eyes off him. If a Sex Magic is attractive, he is usually stunningly so. Sex Magic people often find their way into careers that take full advantage of their beauty and charisma, like modeling or acting.

Whatever they decide to do, Sex Magics need only to be clear about what they want and make any movement in that direction. Once they have intention, the pathway to what they want is usually quite effortless. Where Sex Magic people get themselves into the most trouble is when they are not clear about their own motivations. When their motives are not clear to them, they can easily get caught in a trap of attracting things for the wrong reasons. Out of need for security, they may marry for money but find themselves deeply unhappy as a result. A Sex Magic's competitiveness may cause him to attract a mate with whom he has nothing in common, simply because she is very desirable to others. Sexual attraction and deep infatuation usually rush up upon Sex Magics and prompt them to form bonds rather hastily. For this reason they often find themselves wishing they had taken more time to get to know their partners before getting so deeply involved.

The old adage, "be careful what you ask for" is especially true for Sex Magics. If they lack clarity, they often attract what they do not want, especially unwanted attention. Stalking Sex Magics love to be in the spotlight. Dreaming Sex Magics like the spotlight only when they choose it, and when they do not want it, they may attempt to be invisible. Sex Magic celebrities find themselves the subject of sensational news reporting while celebrities of different magics never seem to attract much press at all, and not because their lives are any less sensational than the Sex Magic's life. They simply do not draw the attention that Sex Magic attracts.

Sex Magic people often have issues about sex. Their precocious sensuality may be threatening to their families and therefore suppressed or discouraged. Or they may have attracted the attention of a sexual predator. They may experiment with sex at a very early age and dabble in careers associated with the sex industry. Whatever the case, their sexuality is often the subject of great concern among their intimates who often confuse their need for sexual expression as a sign of immorality or psychological problems. Needless to say, they need to choose partners with care so that they are not exploited. They also need to understand that they can easily become the object of jealousy if a partner is insecure.

If a Sex Magic is out-of-power, he may become very promiscuous in an attempt to feel powerful. This behavior may become addictive to the point that the Sex Magic engages in sexually exploitive or high-risk behavior because he cannot feel powerful any other way. He may feel compelled to collect a large group of partners in order to shore up his sagging self-esteem. Or he may be tempted to exert control over others, manipulating them by granting or denying them sex.

What Sex Magic people must ultimately come to terms with is this: Sex Magic is not really about sex, even though sex is the easiest way to express it. What Sex Magic is really about is the power to attract, and in so doing, harness creative energy. When a Sex Magic learns to focus on the feeling experience she wants to create, she can prevent herself from attracting out of neediness or ego, and instead use her creative powers to create fulfillment and satisfaction. Because she is so adventurous, the Sex Magic can learn to set her sights on things that most people would not even think possible. She can put together a life that is rich in romantic settings, unusual professions, and fascinating partners and friends.

Exotic combinations of place and profession that might seem out of reach to others are usually no problem at all for a Sex Magic. You might find her in the Caribbean, sunbathing by day and teaching Tango by night. Or you might find she has taken her love of dogs to Alaska where she earns her living raising Malamutes and competing in sledding races. You might find her in some exquisitely remote location in the South Pacific acting as a translator for well-heeled tourists. If she is performing a traditional job, it will usually be in an unusual setting. She might be a secretary in an Embassy in a foreign country or a doctor on a cruise ship. Whatever you find her doing, it is bound to be non-traditional, a little bit risky, and more than a little enviable.

A Sex Magic's body is like a magnet for experience. When a Sex Magic is in present time, his body is like a finely tuned instrument that generates the experiences he wants to create. Sex Magic people are intensely physical, even if their physiques are frail. The body is always of interest to a Sex Magic, and he will often be drawn to professions associated with it, like massage therapy, weight lifting, or bodywork. Sex Magic people have an instinct for knowing how energy moves in the body, and when they feel blocked, they need to move their bodies. They benefit enormously from body movement regimens like tai chi, martial arts, and gymnastics, and they are excellent teachers of yoga, dancing, and aerobics.

When a Sex Magic is afraid, she leaves her body and goes into her head. The minute she does that, she feels like a caged animal, pacing back and forth, looking for an avenue of escape. When she gets in this frame of mind, she makes herself vulnerable to attack by those who would insist that her unconventionality is the source of her problems. If she listens to her detractors, she might easily find herself attracting a traditional job for the sake of security, then sinking into a depression because the job stifles her and makes her feel claustrophobic.

Because their unconventionality makes them subject to criticism, censure, and even attack, Sex Magics need to place themselves in an environment that honors their sensuality, non-traditional style, and uniqueness. When they forget how to create, or remain too long in a situation where they are rejected, they will suffer massive mood swings and periods of deep despair. Their need for attention must be modulated so that they do not become addicted to the attention they attract. If they allow attention to become a substitute for self-esteem, they may desire fame or notoriety out of insecurity, wanting the adoration of many because the unconditional love of one person does not satisfy them. Sex Magics can be vulnerable to their own vanity. If they do not have a strong sense of self, they can come to believe that image is what opens doors for them. If this goes on for too long, they can lose their sense of identity in the pursuit of personas instead of building self-awareness. If a Sex Magic cannot handle the attention she attracts, she may cover up her sexuality or make her appearance unattractive.

Stalking Sex Magics may find themselves betrayed by their own sexual and creative prowess. They are fiercely competitive, and tend to alienate those around them with their superior attitude. They may have difficulty with self-examination, and often dismiss the reactions they engender, chocking it up to jealousy, stupidity, or insecurity on the part of those who have trouble dealing with the intensity of their energy. When a Stalking Sex Magic creates a relationship with someone who cannot honor her for who she is, she may find herself adopting a more acceptable persona in order to keep the peace. She may sabotage her appearance, mute her voice, or try to be more conventional. If this goes on for very long, she may begin to lose touch with how creative she is and feel hopelessly trapped.

Dreaming Sex Magics tend to be swallowed up in their relationships. They often lack a sense of self and may assume various personas over the course of their lives. A Dreaming Sex Magic will often develop her appearance and attributes as if she were writing about a character in a book. While this may enhance her sense of romance, it can be quite debilitating for her relationships. When she assumes an identity because she feels it would be more enchanting or seductive, she loses her sense of self and risks becoming a shell of a person whose artifice and superficiality preclude any honest relating. In fact, her loss of identity may actually cause the rejection she seeks to avoid because there is nothing real to which her partner and friends can relate.

Sex Magic people create most effectively when they feel passion for what they do. When they discover what their passion is, creating it is simply a matter of staying in present time. When they learn to honor their passions, they use their creative power productively, and what they create will feel as good as sex! When they understand that their purpose is to be in the creative flow, they can begin to realize the magnitude of their power to attract what they want.

Sex Magic is one of the most useful magics to employ and can be used to attract everything from financial resources to soulmates. It has a host of practical uses in everyday life. Almost any larger vision can use a little Sex Magic to attract elements needed to support it. For example, if you are trying to create a business, you will want to use Sex Magic to attract clients, employees, service providers, and resources. If you are looking for a new place to live, Sex Magic is the perfect tool for attracting the right home, landlord, and location. Sex Magic should be used whenever you need charisma or spontaneity. For this reason, it is a great magic to employ in situations where you need to loosen up or feel a sense of adventure.

VOID TRAVELING

Power: to know

Purpose: to have free access to all that is knowable by humanity

Gifts: psychic intuition, command of information, curiosity, ability to persuade

Void Travelers are so-called because they can enter the void and travel through it on their search for information. This talent makes Void Travelers very psychic, and their ability to read the matrix can be astonishingly accurate. They also make excellent spiritual mediums, but they are usually good at any profession that is based on the collection, assimilation, and use of information, such as psychiatry, medicine, or science.

Void Magic people are often highly intelligent and love to talk about what they know. It is often through discussion that they do their most productive Void Traveling. As a Void Magic explores ideas, his consciousness is moving through the void to find new information that is linked to the information he may already have. Void Travelers will often have a desire to know something, only to find on the following day that they learn about a book or an article that contains the information they seek.

Void Magics create through knowing what to do. If they do not know what to do, they feel extremely frustrated and powerless. This frustration is part of what drives them to amass vast storehouses of knowledge on many subjects. They are often attracted to metaphysics because of its promise of access to knowledge that cannot be gleaned by ordinary means. When a Void Magic wants to create something, the first thing he does is gather information. If he can remain in present time, his access to exactly what he needs will be forthcoming. If he indulges in fear-based thinking and begins to worry about making a mistake, no amount of information will ever satisfy him, and his search for it will be an unending obstacle to his progress. If he is very out-of-power, he may stifle his intuition and become obsessed with information as an antidote to his fear.

Void Magic people have a *need* to know. Their houses are usually full of books on a wide variety of subjects, but only those subjects that intrigue them. If a Void Traveler is interested in metaphysics, which many of them are, his library will rival any New Age bookstore. In fact, Void Magic people may even write books on subjects they have studied, but about which not much information exists. This is because providing information to others is just as important to them as acquiring it. They often believe that if others simply knew what they know, all problems would be solved. For this reason, Void Magic people usually have issues about their infallibility. They have a strong desire to be right about the subjects they command. This can make them a little overbearing and defensive when challenged. If they are out-of-power, they may avoid endeavors that they might not be able to master with information.

A Void Magic's lessons typically revolve around control. Void Magics may find that their formative life events happened when they were at the mercy of the controlling or bizarre behavior of others. Their parents may have been quite mean, vindictive, or even psychotic, and their relationships later in life tend to reflect whatever coping mechanisms they devised in response to the cruelty they endured. Dreaming Void Magics may hold themselves aloof from others, hesitate to get involved, and use distancing behaviors as a substitute for boundaries. Stalking Void Magics typically try to control everything in their lives: partners, children, friends, business associates, clients, and even the environment where they live or work, in an effort to avoid what they do not want. If a Void Magic does not pro-actively learn her lessons about control, her life will usually slam her into a brick wall where she will be forced to let go of control if she is to survive.

Dreaming Void Travelers need to learn how to maintain their psychic space without resorting to behaviors that distance them from others. They need to learn to address their conflicts and not brush them under the carpet. If left to fester, their unresolved animosity can make them very unpleasant company. Stalking Void Magics need to learn to respect the psychic space of others, and not to engage in psychic snooping or inflict their superior knowledge on others in order to force things to be done their way. Most importantly, they must learn not to dump their frustration and anger on those around them. The force of it is much more overwhelming than they realize and can often damage relationships irrevocably.

It is ironic that Void Magic people, given their extraordinary intellects, are usually plagued by one or more glaring personal blind spots. A Void Traveler's self-awareness can actually be quite absent in places, especially if she has come to rely on her intellect and has stopped engaging in her learning process. In fact, Void Magics often come to believe that their spiritual homework is complete, that they have arrived at full self-awareness. This can leave their intimates speechless because it is blatantly obvious that the blind spot is there, sticking out like a sore thumb. For all of their amazing intelligence, they can be mind-bogglingly dense about the most simple, practical matters that are quite obvious to the average person.

Dreaming Void Magics are very skilled at getting other people to buy into their illusions. They will often use Void Magic's power of persuasion to manipulate the realities of those around them. When those close to them begin to see the cracks in the veneer, out-of-power Dreaming Void Magics will often use emotional smoke and mirrors to distract their intimates from the reality behind the illusion they are projecting. People who have known a Dreaming Void Magic for years may be shocked one day when they discover what has been hidden so effectively from their view.

Void Magic people who are deeply insecure will often appear arrogant, masking their insecurity behind their intellectual superiority. Their ability to read the matrix of others makes them quite skilled at pressing emotional buttons, and when provoked, the out-of-power Void Magic will not hesitate to use sensitive information as a weapon for control. Once the damage is done, she will invariably justify her actions as being for her opponent's own good.

Stalking Void Magics are some of the most capable people you will ever meet. They can accomplish things that most people would never dare attempt. They will often tackle projects that are way beyond them when they start, but they use the challenge to bring their skills and knowledge up to whatever levels are necessary to accomplish what they set out to do. If they are out-of-power, however, they may never start important projects because of their need to control the outcome. They may be unable to discern how much information is enough and continue stockpiling more information than they need out of fear that they will not know something, the need for which they cannot foresee.

Dreaming Void Magics usually have rare and special capacities. Their intuitive gifts are often quite amazing, but if they are not careful, they may lean on a certain specialty and not develop other equally useful gifts. Dreaming Void Travelers have a very difficult time planning anything and often find themselves going in circles when they try. They work best from very general or sketchy plans that allow them to use their intuition to discover the steps involved as they arise.

Stalking Void Travelers very often pick Dreaming Time Magics for their mates because they are very attracted to the Time Magic's patience and calming energy. But often these relationships suffer because the impatient, agenda-driven Void Magic, who knows exactly what to do, may become frustrated with the Dreaming Time Magic's being approach to life. If the Stalking Void Magic pushes too hard, her Dreaming Time Magic mate will likely withdraw from her both sexually and emotionally in an effort to protect his psychic space. Frustrated and hurt, the Stalking Void Magic may resort to provocative behavior, shame, or blame in order to get a rise out of her Dreamer mate and force him to act. This, of course, drives him further into his shell and eventually destroys the relationship by convincing the Time Magic that it is entirely unsafe to express any feelings at all. But long after the relationship is finished, the Stalking Void Magic and the Dreaming Time Magic will stay together, he out of fear of change, and she to maintain her sense of control and avoid feeling powerless to make her marriage work. If, however, the Stalking Void Magic can learn to set aside her agenda and allow her mate to create by being instead of doing—and if the Dreaming Time

Magic can learn to say *no* when his boundaries are being overrun—this combination can be extraordinarily close and mutually supportive.

Dreaming Void Magics tend to have love that is unrequited and may carry a torch for years, with no encouragement from their love interest. They may hang onto feelings for ex-partners long after divorce or estrangement. They may have a short blissful relationship that they feel can never be repeated with another. If this belief causes them to lose touch with their dreams for a relationship, they may be prompted to settle for something much less than they really want or decide to live alone. If the Dreaming Void Magic can stay in touch with the dream he holds in his heart, he can usually find a soulmate waiting for him in the wings. After years of pursuing a love that is unrequited or long since a thing of the past, it might be the person whom he least expects but may have known for some time.

Boredom is a Void Magic's worst enemy. They are typically so intelligent that they become restless without stimulation. They may seek out risky encounters or even provoke conflict just to relieve their boredom. If, however, they use their quiet time to pursue new knowledge or fresh experiences, they can channel their energy into creative self-expression.

All Void Magics need to take care that they do not make assumptions. Their intellects are so quick and their command of information so powerful, they often fail to actually look at the energy of a situation before proceeding because they assume they already have it figured out. They are often afraid to humble themselves before those they believe to be less intelligent or knowledgeable than they are, and they may miss much that these people might have to offer them. In fact, an out-of-power Void Magic is often so judgmental that she fails to notice most of what a person is really all about. If she is not aware of this tendency, she may begin to believe in her snap decisions about people and circumstances, and thereby sever her connection to her magic and the vast resources available to her in the void. When Void Magics are out-of-power they can become quite brooding and negative. They tend to have persecution complexes and have difficulty taking responsibility for the ill will they themselves have engendered with their controlling or distancing behavior.

Void Travelers are at the peak of their creativity when they learn to surrender their personal will to a higher one. When they are in present time, they are capable of knowing anything that is knowable by humanity, and if they work closely with their spirit guides, they have access to knowledge above and beyond what is available to them through their already extraordinary intuitive gifts. Void Magic people need to trust that the knowledge is there and that it will find its way to them. They need to cultivate patience and resist fretting, chafing, or putting their lives on hold. Instead they need to allow for energies, situations, and resources to mature in the fullness of time while they get on with their lives.

Void Magic people may have several highly successful careers, multiple businesses, or several jobs that they juggle at one time. If they pursue higher education, they do so masterfully, and they are often at the top of the class. They usually make full use of every scrap of knowledge they have gained along the way, but often long after the knowledge was acquired. They can be like walking encyclopedias, able to instantly retrieve the most obscure bit of knowledge. Because they rarely forget anything that they learn, their endeavors are usually quite rich in scope and detail. When Void Travelers learn the lesson of boundaries, and surrender their personal will to a higher one, they shine like stars. Their brilliance can be shared with others to amazing effect, and the contribution they make to the greater good can be awe-inspiring. When they can learn to travel the void in present time, their natural genius and curiosity are magnified, and their accomplishments can be truly groundbreaking.

When information is what you need, Void Magic is the answer. It is a fabulous tool for research, investigation, and compiling of data. If you need to know something that is not knowable in the ordinary way, Void Magic will assist your intuition and give you greater ability to find information and guidance from the higher realms. If you are trying to connect with psychic information, guides, or those who have crossed over into Spirit, Void Magic is the ideal tool for making your channel stronger. Void Magic is also very good at sorting out fact from fiction, and reality from denial. It will not only assist you in finding out what you need to know, it will help you be magnetic to sources of information that you seek.

STILLNESS MAGIC

Power: *to see divinity*

Purpose: *to see the Creator at work in all things*

Gifts: *faith, ability to give comfort and encouragement to those who are suffering, ability to discern the nature of divinity*

A Stillness Magic creates through lifting his consciousness to the level of his own divinity where he can witness himself and others as divine spiritual beings. Stillness Magics have the ability to lend a deeply touching spiritual meaning to the most tragic or terrible circumstances, and they are very gifted at elevating the perspective of those who undergo these traumatic events. Of all the magics, it is Stillness Magic that is most inclined to help others and ease suffering. Stillness Magic people usually have very strong faith and feel they have a deeply personal relationship with the Creator. They feel they have direct access to the Creator's power. When they can be still in present time, this access is open to them, and their awareness of their own divinity and their relationship to the Creator places them in the flow. When they are in the flow, their endeavors are upheld in even the most desperate of circumstances.

If a Stillness Magic is out-of-power, she is anything but still. In fact, if she is afraid for herself or another, you will find her franticly throwing everything she knows at the problem. She may spend hours praying for happy outcomes for her troubled loved ones. She may recite lengthy lists of complicated affirmations written to cover every conceivable thing that might go wrong. She may arrive with armloads of self-help books or articles on the problem that concerns her or someone she likes. You are likely to find her hovering over someone she is trying to help, desperate to assist in any way she can, and deluging her charge with suggestions from her well-stocked bag of solutions. Because her suggestions are often quite impractical, she may get her feelings hurt when her well-intentioned offer of support is met with a blank look. No matter how unsuccessful her previous attempts, she is always trying new things, hoping to find the silver bullet that will swiftly vanquish what she fears.

What the Stillness Magic is really doing by all this flurry of activity is running from her own fears of abandonment. In fact, this fear is often a hallmark of the Stillness Magic's character. Fear of abandonment may cause Stillness Magic people to go to extraordinary lengths to remain in the good graces of their intimates. They very often have no clear sense of how much help is appropriate and how much is too much. While their efforts are often nobly selfless, they can easily degrade into behavior that is self-deprecating or overly generous. They may try to care-take those who do not want it and get their feelings hurt when their generosity and concern are rebuffed.

Stillness Magic people often have abandonment as a feature of their childhoods. A parent may have walked out when the Stillness Magic was a child, or the parent may have abandoned the child emotionally, making him feel unwanted or a burden. His parents may have had little time for him or treated him as a nuisance. He may have undergone a severe trauma that was dismissed as trivial or unimportant, leaving him no outlet to express his fear and no assistance with resolving it. He may have been shamed for his fears. Or he might have been deeply intimidated by his parents, afraid that they would not take care of him if he did not go out of his way to please or obey them.

Stillness Magics often place great importance on even their most casual relationships. They may not be terribly selective about who they allow to be close to them, and they may gravitate toward needy or desperate people because this fulfills their need to help. They are often deeply co-dependent, and because they are attracted to those who have little to give, their friendships often serve only to heighten their abandonment fears. In any event, Stillness Magic people often have conflicted relationships. They may have some clues about the nature of the problem, but their fear of abandonment will usually prompt them to stay in any relationship, no matter how one-sided, unsatisfying, or abusive. They are often drawn to relationships with people who are distant, cold, or unpredictable. They may tolerate exploitation because they feel it puts them in a more secure position and reduces the risk that their exploiters will abandon them.

Denial is very common in out-of-power or deeply fearful Stillness Magics, and it is often so strong that people close to them may feel frustrated by their seeming unwillingness to move forward with their own growth. They quite often have difficulty facing unpleasant facts and will sometimes go to great lengths to convince anyone who challenges them that the facts are wrong. The out-of-power Stillness Magic may even engage in counter-phobic behavior, subjecting himself to unnecessary risk in order to prove that he is not afraid. He may be deeply religious or even join a cult in the hope that doing so will make him more pleasing to the Creator who he may unconsciously fear will abandon him.

Anxiety is a feature of the life of most Stillness Magic people. When they are worrying, they tend to whip themselves into a frenzy and make themselves sick with fear. For this reason they may avoid reality, putting off anything that might challenge their tenuous grasp on what they prefer to think or believe. If challenged, they can exhibit a great deal of anger and will often resort to shame or intimidation to dissuade honest feedback. They may under-achieve in an effort to remain in an environment that does not challenge them very much. If they do wind up in a challenging environment, they may quit if they are not allowed to work with minimal supervision and few demands.

If someone has high expectations of a Stillness Magic, she may sabotage the effort in order to prevent further pressure on her to perform. Because she is always offering to help and very eager to volunteer, this behavior can be very confusing for those who are counting on her. She may earn a reputation for being unreliable because her impulse to volunteer and be liked for doing so momentarily overrides her aversion to pressure. This aversion ultimately surfaces and creates misunderstandings and disappointment in those who were counting on the Stillness Magic to do what she promised. She may find their reaction very confusing and feel misunderstood. This may be because half the time she has forgotten the details of what she promised after the flush of praise for volunteering has worn off.

Out-of-power Stillness Magics not only feel a lot of guilt, they are very good at making those around them feel it acutely. One of the reasons they are attracted to religion and spiritual pursuits is for the redemption of guilt that religion may offer them. When confronted with a grievance against him, the Stalking Stillness Magic may appear to run away from responsibility for his actions. What he is actually running from is the debilitating impact that guilt will have on him. He may turn the tables on someone who reproves him, making it the other person's fault and dismissing any legitimate complaint that person may have. However, Dreaming Stillness Magics are far more likely to collapse into a tortured state where they flagellate themselves for offenses they have grossly exaggerated. This may cause those around them to avoid confronting them so as to avoid the high drama of their overreaction. Stalking Stillness people are often quick to feel wronged and may retaliate with unexpected forcefulness. The Dreaming Stillness, on the other hand, often plays the role of the martyr, doling out hefty doses of guilt to those whom she believes have wronged her. In either case, the out-of-power Stillness Magic tends to overreact and take things very personally. They may even feel personally singled out by such impersonal institutions as the government, the legal system, their religion, or the community.

Stillness Magic people have a very high tolerance for emotional and physical pain. They often neglect their health and will put up with chronic pain and other health problems just to avoid being confronted with an unpleasant truth. They confound their intimates by, on the one hand, giving fervent testimony to their faith in the Creator, and on the other hand, behaving as if they have no support whatsoever with everyday life's challenges and crises. Stillness Magics, no matter how competent, may harbor fears that they cannot take care of themselves, that they cannot live without a partner, or that the job they hate is the only option they have open to them. Dreaming Stillness Magics often have deep-seated fears for their personal safety and can be terrified to drive on freeways or ride in airplanes. They often suffer from anxiety disorder but may refuse help because they believe their anxiety protects them by alerting them to all the potential dangers. They may avoid groups or classes for fear of being called upon and not having the answer, or for fear of having their answers or remarks challenged.

In spite of their obvious lack of maturity in some areas, Stillness Magic people are capable of exceptional clarity. When they are in a state of stillness, their understanding of the Creator is deeply moving and reassuring. When they are in the present moment, Stillness Magic people have a certainty about divinity that can open the doors of Creation and make the Creator real and accessible to others. They have great power to help others deal with life's uncertainties and to assist those around them in seeing the divinity within themselves and at work in the circumstances. They may be drawn to religious orders, but they also excel at any of the helping professions, like counseling, coaching, nursing, parenting, and care-giving. Stalking Stillness Magics often make excellent politicians and sales people because their genuine concern for others is very appealing. Many Dreaming Stillness Magics are too fearful or sensitive to do very well in the work-a-day world, but they are often truly gifted artists. So instead, they may make their living as artists or in highly skilled crafts requiring artistic ability, where they are shielded from the rigors of office politics or pressure to perform.

Stillness Magics need to learn to face their fears and stop running from challenges and painful facts. If they can learn to be still and live in the truth of their relationship with the Creator, what they fear will be revealed for what it is, an illusion with no substance. They need to learn that everyone gets what is truly needed, themselves included, and that the world does not rest on their shoulders. In short, they need to learn to let go and let the Creator do what their faith informs them.

When Stillness Magics are in power, their contribution to the evolution of consciousness is unrivaled. They inspire people to love one another, to be kind and generous, and to live in the full awareness of themselves as divine spiritual beings. In-power Stillness Magics have unshakable faith, and this makes them invincible in the face of adversity. Their faith can carry them through any situation, and their innate goodness of heart can inspire even the most selfish person to give a little of himself. When a Stillness Magic is in present time, he knows to pray, not out of fear, but out of his sheer joy in knowing the Creator has a unique role for him in the infinite scheme of Creation.

Stillness Magic is invaluable when you need faith. This faith can take a variety of forms, such as faith that everything will work out, even if you cannot see how that will be. It can give you faith in yourself, helping you to take risks that are appropriate to actualizing your dreams. Stillness Magic can also help you detach from the problems of others by assisting you in seeing that everyone is divine and has his own spiritual path. It can be a great comfort when you are faced with world events because it explains suffering in the context of sacrifice and ultimate evolution to a higher consciousness. Stillness Magic can also help you be still instead of frantic. It can allow you to know the Creator is there for you and for others, furthering your evolution and offering you the potential to fill your life with joy, creativity, and ease.

PHOENIX MAGIC

Power: *to transform*

Purpose: *to be a catalyst for change*

Gifts: *self-examination, transformation, ability to reform outworn structures*

Phoenix Magic people create by transforming energy. They are rarely content to leave things as they are and feel compelled to constantly improve themselves, their surroundings, and the people in their lives. They routinely act as a catalyst for transformation in their relationships, their work, and in the community. They typically undergo metamorphosis a number of times in their lives, making radical shifts in careers, lifestyles, and social groups, often without warning.

Phoenix Magic is about embracing the cycle of death and rebirth. If this is not honored, and the Phoenix Magic puts off needed change, he will find his life reduced to rubble. But not to worry, given time to regroup, the Phoenix Magic will usually rise from ruins stronger, wiser, and more successful than he was before. This is because destruction frees the Phoenix Magic to transform what is no longer appropriate and create himself anew.

Phoenix Magics cannot be reborn until they allow the death of the outworn to occur. If they are out-of-power, they may linger in the death cycle. This usually happens when the Phoenix Magic has no clear idea what he will become when he completes his metamorphosis. Once his idea is clear to him, he will make the transformation quite readily. The problem is, if he becomes impatient, he may make up a vision that is not appropriate for him and undergo the transformation only to find that he must immediately destroy what he has built and start over again. But more often than not, the Phoenix Magic needs to stop judging the destruction of his creations as something bad. If he judges them as bad, he may begin to view his life as a series of failures or feel that he is always thwarted in his attempts to create. He may come to believe himself incapable of creating what he wants. If he adopts this attitude, he cuts himself off from the secret to his creative power: the cycle of death and rebirth.

Phoenix Magic people are both a wonder and a puzzle to their intimates. Everyone who knows them well understands their remarkable ability to transform anything they set their hearts upon. What baffles them is the way the Phoenix Magic is continually blowing up her life and starting over, then complaining about her lack of security and stability. If her intimates do not understand the principles of Phoenix Magic, they will probably beg her to settle down and stop making the waves that ultimately wash over and crush her. What they do not realize is that the Phoenix Magic is compelled to create change whenever she sees that change is necessary or would improve things.

Phoenix Magic's biggest hot button is justice. They often see their childhoods as unfair, and may feel cheated or passed over for others who were no more worthy, on merit, than they were. They may find that they are unjustly accused of having unsavory motives they do not have, or doing things they did not do. They often attract circumstances that inflame their life-long sense of being treated unfairly. If they are Stalkers, this sense of injustice can be greatly magnified by the Stalker's acute sensitivity to being wronged.

Inequity often marks the life of the Phoenix Magic. He may have trouble deciding what is fair and will often sell himself short in transactions and agreements. His sense of justice is so strong that he will often prefer to weight the deal heavily in favor of the other person, just be sure that he is being fair. He will often offer more than he should, only to find later that he resents the imbalance in the agreement that he himself has created.

Phoenix Magic people need to tread lightly with their families and close associates who quickly grow weary of the Phoenix Magic's desire to reshape and reform them. Phoenix Magic people may find their all-too-good advice rejected out of hand simply because those around them are sick of being told that they need to improve themselves. This is matter of great confusion to the Phoenix Magic who cannot understand why anyone would not welcome an opportunity to make things better. They may not realize that they are constantly fixing what is not broken, and that not all change is necessarily an improvement.

Phoenix Magic people excel in any endeavor where they can utilize their ability to catalyze change. They make very successful interior decorators, hair designers, estheticians, and consultants, where their advice on change is both needed and welcomed. They also make very good motivational speakers because they know instinctively how to inspire others to transform their own lives. You will find many of them in the self-help industry, assisting others in evolving, growing, and creating transformation. While they are very attracted to the helping professions, they tend to shy away from jobs that would lock them into a routine, unless the work itself is constantly posing new and different challenges. For this reason they are outstanding in fields like cosmetic surgery, and any other profession associated with restoration or renewal.

Phoenix Magics are often Renaissance people. Because they love change, they may master many skills and do so many things well that they have a difficult time choosing what to do. When they learn a new skill, they will not be satisfied until they master it, and when they achieve mastery, they will more than likely move on to something new. Skills they have mastered and left behind will often serve them well later in life when they enter a new field or direction where that skill might be put to good use. They are very resourceful and are always thinking about what resources could be applied to create more change, more rapidly and more effectively.

If a Phoenix Magic encounters a situation in her job or relationship that demands necessary change, but she is somehow restricted from making it, she will probably call it quits. If she is a Stalker, the end will come swift and furious. If a Dreamer, there will probably be plenty of warnings, but once a Phoenix Magic makes her decision to leave, there will be no going back, even if she attempts to do so out of fear. This is because the Phoenix Magic has only two choices: transform or die.

Phoenix Magics can make very difficult partners in relationships and in business. They are never content to leave well enough alone and are always looking with an eye to improve whatever is there. They often find themselves at the center of a controversy that results from their attempt to transform something that others may want to leave unchanged. Because their professional lives suffer cyclical periods of chaos, their mates can find themselves cringing when they start to hear the first complaints the Phoenix Magic makes when change she desires is either halted or thwarted. If the Phoenix Magic is out-of-power, this chronic complaining may deeply frustrate her mate who may feel that she should learn to live with things as they are. But if a Phoenix Magic decides to remain in a job she detests for the sake of security, her health will be the first sacrifice.

This is because the Phoenix Magic will begin to manifest the death cycle in her own body. In fact, many Phoenix Magics find the body and the material plane so limiting that they actively contemplate hastening their transformation into Spirit. It is not necessarily that they have been driven to despair, although that sometimes is the case. It is more that they find the earth-plane to be a dense and difficult place, where change is sluggish and the population seems hopelessly stuck in unconsciousness. For this reason, it is crucial that Phoenix Magics create spiritual community or they may come to believe that they do not belong here.

One area that concerns Phoenix Magics is their friendships. While they can maintain committed relationships with a partner, they often have trouble keeping friends. This may be very confusing to them since Phoenix Magic people tend to make friends quite easily. What they do not realize is that their very energy is a catalyst for change, and if they choose to associate with people who are not on a path of intense personal growth, the implicit demand for change may ultimately create a conflict that results in an irreconcilable rift. If a Phoenix Magic tries to transform a relationship with a partner who is unwilling, the relationship will quickly become an albatross around her neck, weighting her down with the burden of pulling the reluctant party forward when he really does not want to come.

An out-of-power Stalking Phoenix tends to be overly tolerant in the early stages of a friendship. This usually backfires when her patience ultimately begins to grow thin. When she is convinced that the transgressions have finally tipped the scales, and her fairness could not possibly be questioned, she usually sheds the relationship quickly, feeling little obligation to explain. This can be confusing for the friend, especially when the relationship is a long-term one that the friend had come to think of it as permanent. The friend may have no idea that the behavior that was once tolerated is now the source of friction.

A Dreaming Phoenix Magic tends to lose herself in relationships, and may slavishly serve a partner or friend, hoping that her dedication will effect the necessary change. Her reluctance to confront may cause her to bear the whole burden, shore up the relationship, and keep it afloat at great cost to herself. Dreaming Phoenix Magics may convince themselves that it is commitment that keeps them in a relationship, but fear of doing their partner an injustice is the more likely reason. Dreaming Phoenix Magics are often manipulated by partners who play victim, and they may have a difficult time recognizing how grossly out of balance the relationship really is. Because they have such a deep need to be fair, they may sacrifice their own happiness in order to avoid being accused of perpetrating an injustice. And if they do eventually bring themselves to leave a deeply unhappy marriage, they will often hesitate to take the final legal action.

Phoenix Magics need to learn that people are responsible for deciding upon and implementing whatever changes they themselves see fit. They need to choose their intimates, jobs, and circumstances carefully or they may find their lives become depressingly unstable. A Phoenix Magic may find she is happiest being her own boss because the changes she will undoubtedly need to make cannot be encumbered by a reluctant superior. Phoenix Magic people need to choose professions that are about creating transformation, where they are consulted for their advice, and where they have a great deal of freedom and autonomy.

If a needed change is not readily forthcoming, the Phoenix Magic must willingly enter the death cycle so that he can then be reborn. When the death cycle is upon a Phoenix Magic, he needs to get it over with as quickly as possible, and not delay his transformation out of fear. The consequences of delaying the end of things are almost always worse for the Phoenix Magic than if the change had been made in its proper time. When the demand for change is obvious, the Phoenix Magic has no choice but to answer the call. If he fears change, he is cut off from his magic and will ultimately find himself standing amidst the ruins, wishing he had taken action when he first knew it was needed.

Phoenix Magic's lesson is about embracing change without fear. It is about honoring the dance of death and rebirth that is reflected throughout the entire universe. When a Phoenix Magic understands that his very energy is a catalyst for change, he can begin to apply this energy selectively and employ it where it can do the most good. When he chooses more wisely what to transform and what to leave as it is, he can have enormous impact on those who really want assistance. If he can embrace the cycle of death and rebirth in his own life, he can be a powerful role model and catalyst when change is demanded but those who must make it are hesitating out of fear.

Phoenix Magic is very useful in reorganization, restructuring, and reform. For this reason, it is a very useful tool for self-examination. When you are facing great change, Phoenix Magic can allow you to embrace it with dignity and grace because it informs you of the natural cycle of death and rebirth that is evident throughout Nature. Phoenix Magic is useful in helping you reframe your thoughts, transform stuck emotions, and liberate yourself from the trauma of endings. The mythical Phoenix rose from the ashes of its own destruction more beautiful than it was before. It is a powerful tool for rebuilding your life after tragedy, trauma, or separation from anything you hold dear. Phoenix Magic can give you the courage to move forward and create from a whole new dream.

ILLUMINATION MAGIC

Power: to understand what is real

Purpose: to shed light on truth

Gifts: insight, words that change hearts and minds, ability to attract recognition

The Illumination Magic is a seeker, and this search for truth is usually life-long. Truth is something she studies, and she will go to the ends of the earth to enhance her understanding of what is real. Illumination Magic creates through the use of words, and her words have great power to attract recognition, whether they are spoken or written. This recognition is usually well deserved because the Illumination Magic has amazing clarity to light the way in confusion or difficulty. She is typically an exceptional writer, speaker, and orator, and she will find success in any endeavor that utilizes her verbal gifts.

The early life of Illumination Magics are often characterized by unreasonable rules, restrictions, or punishments, and their parents and caregivers are likely to have been angry or authoritarian. Their parents may have expressed anger through passive-aggression, or they may have been highly volatile and prone to attacks of rage. In any case, Illumination Magic people are usually raised in an atmosphere of control and rigidity. Because Illumination Magics are almost never Stalkers, they learn as children to navigate conflict by trying to understand the other person's point of view. If they are Stalkers, they may fight and struggle to explain their own point of view in the hope that this will loosen the unreasonable restrictions placed on them. When this fails to have any affect, they may attempt to live their lives as Dreamers.

Many Illumination Magics gravitate toward situations that oppress them in their relationships, jobs, and lifestyles, and they often have a great deal of trouble extricating themselves from these things because they are always so acutely aware of both sides of any argument. They may find it much easier to argue the case of their opponents than to defend their own points of view. Although they are masters of clarity when it comes to things outside themselves, they are often muddled and confused about their own problems.

The Illumination Magic will always try to apply reason when he is seeking the truth of something. This may not be very effective in dealing with problems that are close to him because it is very difficult for him to digest the unreasonable. Where a lack of reason lies at the heart of the matter, he may be mystified about how to solve it. While he has incredible ability to reason his way through complex situations and understand them with great clarity, he typically has a great deal of trouble dealing with emotions, both his own emotions and those of persons close to him. If you ask him what he wants, he will probably tell you he wants people to be reasonable so that they too can see the truth.

Illumination Magics are very gentle but rarely shy. They enjoy the company of others and feel very lonely when isolated from their friends. Because they are almost always Dreamers, their natural avoidance of conflict is usually a huge disadvantage in their relationships. If they are Stalkers, they may go through life struggling to reconcile the Illumination Magic's need to keep the peace and the Stalker's need to raise and resolve the conflict. While they often see quite clearly where their own needs are not being met, they may avoid at great cost to themselves the confrontation that might serve to change the situation or free them from it.

Because their understanding of others is so deep, they often feel they have no right to do anything that would hurt someone's feelings or make that person unhappy in any way. They may even engage in extra-marital affairs to get their needs met while they maintain the façade of their dead or dying relationship. If the relationship is in danger of finally falling apart, the Illumination Magic will often make amends, not because he wants to, but because he cannot stand to be the cause of another's suffering. What the Illumination Magic may not admit to himself is that his behavior is actually detrimental to the other person. He may not realize that his actions stifle the growth and evolution of others by preventing them from undergoing discomfort that might lead to greater awareness. In partnerships, he may think of himself as self-sacrificing and noble when all he is really doing is running away from his fear.

Illumination Magics are often deeply philosophical, and because their observations are so astute, their discourses on topics that interest them are fascinating. While their early lives might best be characterized as stifling, their adult lives are usually anything but that. They may wander the world in search of new and interesting points of view on spiritual, philosophical, or political matters. If they are out-of-power, the search can become an addiction, and if they are not self-aware, they may come to find ordinary life quite unsatisfying. This can make them prone to seek excitement rather than fulfillment. This need for excitement may make even the Dreamers among them uncharacteristically impatient and restless. While they may be able to exhibit boundless patience for the foibles of others, they have very little patience for situations they find dull or boring. But because they are most often Dreamers, fear may make it quite difficult for them to take action to change their circumstances. If they are out-of-power, their preoccupation with being liked might prompt them to bury their true feelings and don an artificial mask of niceness that fools no one who knows them well. If they have health problems, they are usually stress-related due to their failure to be honest with themselves and others. This is particularly ironic when you consider that Illumination Magic is all about seeking truth.

Perhaps because their upbringing was so restrictive, fear will often cause Illumination Magics to quit their search for truth and revert to occupations and lifestyles that hem them in and stifle their creativity. If they are out-of-power, their need for security may be triggered if their search takes them a little too far out of their comfort zone. They may harbor a hidden but deep-seated aggression. Because this aggression is something they think of as a threat to reason, they may seek stimulation to cover up these feelings, only to find themselves terrorized by the risk involved. They may spend their entire lives vacillating wildly between excitement and safety, uncertainty and security, to the great confusion of their families and friends who may beg them to settle down and be sensible. This argument is very compelling to the Illumination Magic's high regard for reason, and if he is not careful, he might follow this advice right into a straightjacket of security that he can never live with.

Illumination Magics are very interested in promoting concepts that will help broad groups of people. While their kindness and gentleness make them very good counselors, they prefer to broadcast their message to a much wider audience. They want to operate on the level of shifts in global consciousness, bringing their truth into business, government, and society in order to make these institutions more compassionate and humane. They are at the height of their creativity when they are speaking or writing about their truth, and what they say usually attracts a great deal of recognition. People love listening to them because their perspective is often unique, intriguing, and moving.

Illumination Magics need to learn to be compassionate without compromising their own boundaries. They need to learn to elevate the importance of their own happiness, and not sacrifice it for the sake of keeping the peace. They need to learn that the truth within is more important than any philosophy they seek. They need to speak the truth about their own feelings and desires so that they can be their authentic selves. They can then learn to place their trust in this authenticity, and believe in the truth of their most heart-felt desires. When the Illumination Magic has learned to be in present time and be truthful in his personal life, his understanding of truth in the wider world lights up like a flame, and his words can have an impact he never dreamed possible.

Illumination Magic is very useful if you are helping someone sort out his confusion over complex issues. It is also invaluable when you are writing what you hope will change the way people look at something. Because this magic has great power to change hearts and minds, it is a powerful tool for speech writers and speech makers who want their words to attract and hold the attention of a group. Where Phoenix Magic is useful for self-examination, Illumination Magic is better equipped to gain insight into the behavior of others. It is a particularly powerful tool when the issues of others seem clouded and confused, or when their emotions are high and may be masking the truth. Because Illumination Magic makes words magnetic to recognition, it is invaluable when preparing a manuscript or a proposal for consideration.

HEALING TOUCH

Power: to heal

Purpose: to be a conduit for divine love

Gifts: catalyst for healing body and mind, ability to shift and move energy

Healing Touch Magics create and heal by moving energy in themselves and others, and they are magnificent healers of the body and mind. They are deeply loving and caring, but their intensity can be very off-putting if they are preoccupied with their own concerns. They often have trouble getting close to people, and many find their energy almost nerve-wracking. This can be because the divine love that they channel strips away dishonesty and leaves others feeling exposed and pressured.

Healing Touch Magics actually have the power to bring divine love into their crown centers and move it out through the palms of their hands. Their bodies are conduits for divine love, and they are capable of moving energy in groups of people, just by entering a room. However, if they are out-of-power, their self-absorption can be highly irritating and place rigorous demands on their relationships. In either case, Healing Touch people benefit from closing their chakras and grounding their energy so that they are not broadcasting it with such intensity. They may even find that doing so makes it much easier for them to be in present time.

Healing Touch Magics are usually very powerful, whether Dreamers or Stalkers, and their affection is given generously. But friends may grow to feel that they only hear from the Healing Touch when he wants something. Having a conversation with Healing Touch people can be difficult because their main focus is on themselves and what they are doing with their own healing process or quest for personal growth. They may not realize that this is monotonous because they assume that they are teaching by example, and they are so fascinated by their own process, they cannot imagine that it would not be of interest to someone else. Because they are so focused on themselves, they may miss vital clues to what is going on around them. Conflict often takes them completely by surprise because they were not paying the slightest bit of attention to anything but their own process.

Healing Touch people are always seeking to change their energy and are very attracted to anything they believe will raise their vibration. They often try a number of techniques and may earn the reputation for being dilatants because they sometimes flit from therapy to therapy, never staying with any one technique very long. If out-of-power, they often lack the determination to stick with something long enough to allow it to work. When placed on a program they may find it difficult to comply with the requirements, and they often sabotage themselves, thereby ensuring that their efforts will not be successful.

The early childhood of Healing Touch people is often marked by the influence of deeply fearful parents or parents who terrify them. Their caregivers may have constantly told them to be afraid, to be careful, or to watch out for danger. If their parents were religious, they may have taught them that God will punish them if they are disobedient. Or perhaps parents told the Healing Touch that there is no God. Whatever their religious beliefs, the caregiver of the Healing Touch will very often hold the view that the world is a terrible place where life is ground out one day at a time until death finally ends further suffering. For whatever reason, the Healing Touch often grows up feeling disconnected from the very divine love that is her gift. But eventually she will be drawn to heal that rift and connect with Spirit on her own terms, if only to create a balance for her conditioning. In fact, there is nothing more important to a Healing Touch than balance, and she will do almost anything to achieve it.

The Healing Touch will eventually need to reckon with the fears imparted to him. If he is a Dreamer, he may allow fear to lurk in the shadows and leave him chronically anxious. He will usually counter any suggestion with his fears about it, and he may talk himself out of doing things by imagining the potential for what he fears. If he is a Stalker, he may become very controlling, insecure, and jealous. He may even avoid anything he is not absolutely certain that he can control. He may resort to logic chopping to justify his perceptions, and he may be convinced that this gives him a balanced perspective. The Dreaming Healing Touch may consistently choose whatever middle ground he can devise, not because he believes it is right, but because he believes it is balanced. This can lead him far away from his own authentic center.

When a Healing Touch focuses his energy on performing healing work for others, the intensity with which he does so can create dramatic results. Healing Touch people often earn accolades for being the best at whatever their discipline happens to be. Because their personal relationships tend to be awkward, they will often focus most of their attention on their careers so they can feel competent and have a sense of their power. They may be very good at healing through physical touch, but touching is not necessary. They are also very good at long-distance energy work on individuals. But what they truly excel at is moving energy in groups.

When a Healing Touch is in present time, her influence is deeply grounding. When she has turned her attention from herself to others, the impact she can have is immediately evident. She may be speaking, but what she is actually doing is moving out any energy that the individuals involved are ready to release. This makes her exceptionally good at professions that are associated with empowerment, especially if they have an element of spirituality at their core. Her career may take her through a variety of healing modalities, such as Reiki, EMDR, craniosacral therapy and other techniques that move or release emotional energy in the body. Healing Touch people also make excellent mediators and negotiators of disputes, especially highly charged ones like hostage taking, because they are so skilled at bringing energy into balance.

Healing Touch people can sense energy through their hands. If they are very sensitive, they may actually be able to read a person's energy simply by stepping into that person's aura. When they do touch someone, that person can typically feel energy moving in that part of the body. They are highly perceptive of anything energetic and will immediately notice any change in the energy long before they can interpret what it implies. If they are out-of-touch with their feelings, this may create very high levels of anxiety because they know that something is terribly wrong, but they cannot determine exactly what it is.

Healing Touch parents typically have children who challenge their fear and demand to be unleashed from its control. It is often their children who help them come to grips with their issues by confronting the Healing Touch Magic's anxious perspective. The children of the Healing Touch parent will often force him to take his attention off himself. Other parents may be appalled at the Healing Touch parent's apparent lack of concern about things that ought to be troubling. They may be equally mystified at his over-reaction to things that seem trivial. What may be going here is that the Healing Touch is reading the energy instead of the behavior. He may sense things that are not obvious, and when he knows he has read the energy accurately, he must learn to stand his ground with his detractors, especially with the authorities at school.

If the energy of a situation feels uncomfortable to a Healing Touch, he may wriggle out of it by making excuses. He may do this because explaining the energy may not come easily to him, and he does not want to risk jeopardizing his decision to extricate himself. If his opponent is controlling or persuasive, he may deflect the debate altogether by throwing up a smoke screen that has nothing to do with his real issue. If he is a Stalker, confronting him can be a real challenge because he will likely use a highly-charged emotional decoy to move the argument away from what he is unwilling to address. If he is a Dreamer, he may cloud the issue so completely that his opponent might find himself lost in a fog of hazy or nebulous issues.

Healing Touch Magics are often deeply frustrated. Because their magic is so specialized, they may find it difficult to create for themselves. They are so preoccupied with taking the middle ground, they may not always see the wonderful opportunities that might require a shift off the center to a slightly more risky or even somewhat radical approach. If they focus too intently on their process, they may not see the forest for the trees as they rehash their problems innumerable times. The solution for the Healing Touch is almost always this: convert fear into love.

The Healing Touch Magic who conquers his fear will immediately find love: the divine love of the Creator, love of himself and for his neighbor, and his deep and abiding love of humanity. When the Healing Touch is in-power, he can navigate any waters through the application of the divine love that flows through him. He can then stop looking for the latest technique, skill, or modality, and begin to do what he does best: love with all his heart. When a Healing Touch is in present time, his connection to Spirit upholds him in ways that delight and surprise him. Healing Touch Magics create by moving energy in themselves and in others. When they are in present time and channeling divine love, they can become the architects of enormous shifts in the mass consciousness and truly change the world.

Healing touch is the most powerful tool you have for healing the body or for moving the energy of emotions. Healing Touch is especially useful when injuries, both physical and emotional, require the intervention of divine love. In fact, Healing Touch Magic is the force of intervention that can block negative flows and restore love to a situation. This magic can be used to break deadlocks in negotiations where anger is keeping the parties entrenched. It can be used to diffuse hostility in individuals and in crowds. But it is also useful in healing rifts and settling arguments.

SACRED WEAVING

Power: to connect through Spirit

Purpose: to connect energy, people and ideas in service of the higher good

Gifts: networks that foster healing, creation of sacred space

Sacred Weavers create through making connections. They have a gift for pick-ing up threads and building from them an exquisite tapestry of ideas and people. Sacred Weavers are always Dreamers, and their magic greatly magnifies the quali-ties of Dreaming. In fact, this magic could be considered Dreaming in its purest form. Because they tend to think in pictures, they often have difficulty expressing themselves in words. However, they can speak very articulately if they are using words to describe what they see. In fact, whenever they are communicating, Sacred Weavers do best when their vision is the context for what they are saying. Their visions are often deeply moving and can inspire contribution by others to whatever higher good the Sacred Weaver is trying to uphold.

If most Dreamers have trouble dealing with conflict, no one has greater diffi-culty with it than a Sacred Weaver. When faced with a conflict, his first response is to deny that a conflict exists, and when faced with having to take action that is uncomfortable for him, he will probably do nothing at all. Many Sacred Weavers retreat when the tide of emotions around them is too overwhelming. They feel deeply the feelings of others, and have a great fear of emotional overload. They have difficulty saying *no* to their intimates and may create a good deal of stress for themselves when conflicting emotional demands are made on them. When over-whelmed, they implode, not knowing how to create psychic space for themselves. So instead they may retreat, avoiding contact or averting the subject from any-thing that touches upon their emotions. If their attempts to create psychic space are thwarted, or if they fail to ask for space when they need it, Sacred Weavers can react with surprising animosity. When confronted about this behavior, they will usually deny that there is anything wrong.

Sacred Weavers are always eager to pull new and interesting people into their lives in order to satisfy their deep need for connection. However, they may have difficulty looking ahead or determining how a situation might eventually make them feel. When they are out-of-power, past experience does not seem to teach them very much, and their impulse to connect can get the better of them when their impulses prompt them to get too close, too quickly. If the relationship undergoes stress, they rapidly reach emotional overload and feel a compulsion to make a hasty retreat. This sudden and complete withdrawal usually comes as a total shock to their intimates who see the Sacred Weaver move from loving and welcoming to cold and distancing in the blink of an eye. Their former friends and lovers may accuse them of being narcissistic, but it may be that they simply did not know any other way to create sanctuary for themselves.

When the hand of friendship is extended to them, Sacred Weavers often do not know what to do. If given leads or other opportunities to make important contacts, they may fail to pick up perfectly appropriate threads, but they are just as likely to have so many threads in mind that they cannot choose between them. They may put off connecting so long that opportunities pass them by. Or they might just as easily pick up a thread and quite impulsively weave it into their lives without considering for a moment the profound impact it might have on them or their families.

The childhood of Sacred Weavers is often marked by a feeling of obligation to care for the needs of others. Their parents may have been selfish and needy. These parents may have had trouble meeting the basic emotional needs of the family and left the children to raise themselves. Sacred Weavers typically learn very early in life to give up any hope of having boundaries because they think their own needs will be neglected or overlooked if they do not look after the needs of others. Their caregivers may blatantly demand to be cared for or force the Sacred Weaver to take responsibility for the needs of his siblings. He may grow up deeply resenting anyone who places demands on him but have no idea how to set boundaries or decline inappropriate requests.

Sacred Weavers are often attracted to abusive relationships and may stay in them, remaining in a state of denial about their victimization. They may begin to act out the reality of their situation but be absolutely unconscious about what is happening. In fact, Sacred Weavers often have difficulty separating objective fact from their inner fiction, and they are often devastated when the truth finally penetrates the veil of their denial. What frustrates those closest to them is that they never seem to make the connection between past mistakes and the behavior that created them. If a situation in their past is unpleasant, they will wipe the feelings from memory, and because they very often do not have a clear sense of their personal history, they may be doomed to repeat it.

Sacred Weavers are often deeply co-dependent, not so much out of caring as from a sense of duty. Their intimates often take advantage of them. They may feel compelled to comply with any request but deeply resent it when they do. If they are very out-of-power they may transfer their resentment to someone who has little or nothing to do with their true inner conflict. When they are under emotional pressure, they may be so concerned with avoiding obligations they do not want, that they are headless of the legitimate needs of those around them. They may feel completely unable to balance their own needs with the needs of others when these needs appear to conflict. This can make them seem absurdly self-sacrificing or completely self-absorbed and inconsiderate. But it may be that the Sacred Weaver is simply unable to resolve her inner conflict any other way.

Sacred Weavers are often very psychic but have a tendency to ignore any psychic information that challenges their denial. You often hear them say that they wish they had listened to their inner voice. Their intuition is often remarkably good, but they are usually afraid to follow it. Their dreams are often composed of fantastic images and breathtaking scenes. These dreams may contain dramatic symbolism that can help them greatly on their spiritual journey. They have a very rich symbolic life, but if they are not careful, they can lead themselves down a painful road by believing that something is a sign from Spirit and reading into it meaning that is not there.

Sacred Weavers typically have unusual professions and often find themselves traveling great distances to do their work. They may be connected in every conceivable way to a host of people in every walk of life. They are fascinated by ideas and will often be attracted to professions in world organizations that are based on ideals. They tend to be very idealistic, and their visions for the world are usually quite beautiful and meaningful. They collect unique spiritual and visionary tools, and they like to employ them in their work as well as their personal lives.

Sacred Weavers are at their best when they are making connections, holding the connections together, and passing ideas and concepts through this network. They are at their worst when they try to do the work these ideas suggest because they cannot be in a state of connection and do the work at the same time. If they are out-of-power this can be a huge obstacle for them because the way they deal with conflict often makes it impossible for them to properly supervise the work of others. They may have a very difficult time deciding what to do and, as a result, do nothing at all. They usually benefit from prioritizing their work and learning to discard outworn or outdated ideas. This helps them focus on what is important. They may need to work from scripts when selling their ideas or dealing with situations that make them uncomfortable. If they feel intimidated, they will usually have a great deal of difficulty converting their extraordinary visions into words.

Sacred Weavers often feel discouraged when the fabric of their networks collapse. When this happens, they need to learn to move on and realize that any connection requires two connectors, and if a thread breaks, it is not the end of the world. Weaving is delicate work, and even though a spider's silk is one of the strongest substances on earth, the woven web is really quite fragile. Because her webs are delicate, the Sacred Weaver must learn not to be attached to them, but continue to do what she does best: weaving her connections to create sacred space for herself and others. If she does not learn this, her web can become a trap, snaring her in a tangle of commitments she does not want, and burdening her with the deceptions she uses to avoid them.

Sacred Weavers need to learn that their purpose is to create psychic and sacred space for themselves and others. They must learn to say *no* and allow those around them to grow and learn from experience. They need to learn to value their own needs for space, solitude, and sanctuary, and to choose their threads wisely. Once a thread is chosen, Sacred Weavers must learn to take action, weaving it into its appropriate place, the place that matches their vision of higher good. When they do this, they can begin to take joy in their connections and build networks that foster healing, growth, and world change.

Sacred Weaving is very useful in building groups and organizations that serve a higher purpose. It is a powerful tool for creating networks that transmit ideas and connect people who share a common interest in something that serves the higher good. If you are trying to create sanctuary, there is no more effective tool than Sacred Weaving to create psychic space that provides shelter against turbulent emotional energy, yet still lets in spiritual light and air.

Co-creating Your Life with Spirit

Co-creating your life with Spirit is about harnessing the alchemy that occurs when you are deeply and authentically yourself in present time, guided by your life purpose, and moving in the direction of your dreams. When you are in present time and living your desire for essence, magic in all of its forms is immediately accessible to you. The natural resonance between what you desire and who you are is what sets up the perfect conditions for spiritual alchemy, and your desire for essence becomes a focus for your power to co-create with the power of Spirit.

Alchemy—or the performing of magic—was once characterized as bringing certain elements together to create a reaction that turns a base metal into gold. Spiritual alchemy is the process by which you bring the power of magic together with a higher purpose in present time. Feeling the truth of your creative power is the most authentic emotion you can experience, and when you do, you generate a flow of energy that harnesses your power and makes it available for co-creation. When you create with spiritual alchemy, you unleash limitless alchemical possibilities that can infuse your desire for essence with life force and birth it into being.

Each magic has a higher purpose and a power that flows from that purpose. Each magic also has gifts that make it appropriate for use in certain circumstances and less so in others. When you state the power of *any* magic, it rings true to the core of your being.

Your primary personal magic and life purpose are the keys to being your authentic self, and they are usually the most appropriate tools for creating your authentic life. For example, if you are a Phoenix Magic, you will naturally gravitate toward transformation, and your life purpose no doubt contains language that reflects your desire to act as a catalyst for change in your own life, the lives of others and in the world. If you are a Stillness Magic, your authentic life will always focus on your faith, and your purpose will probably include helping others have faith and greater awareness of their own divinity. When you bring any higher purpose together with magic in present time, you can use the alchemical energy that is generated to create your soul's desires. When you energize the desires of the soul rather than the needs of Mind, the forms you birth into being create your authentic life, a life that perfectly reflects who you are as a soul.

When you examine what you are attempting to create, you may recognize that some elements of the vision are better supported by the use of a magic that is not your primary one. It may be that creating has been a struggle for you simply because the gifts of your magic are not well suited to manifesting certain very specific things. For example, if you are a Void Magic, creating relationships might prove rather difficult because your tendency to rely on what you already know may be counter-productive to being open to another's point of view. If you are a Healing Touch, finances may prove a struggle because the divine love you channel does not concern itself with material needs.

Fortunately, you are not limited to your primary personal magic. You already use other magics, and you probably have a secondary magic in which you have developed a high level of skill. For example, you might be a Stalker who cultivated a skill in Time Magic in order to give yourself more patience and the ability to relax and do nothing once in a while. You might be a Sacred Weaver who employs Stillness Magic to help you accept the occasional collapse of sacred space and encourage you to keep weaving.

Each magic has gifts that make it appropriate for creating certain things. If you want to attract something you need, Sex Magic is an excellent tool for doing that. If you want to transform something, like a bad habit or a pattern of reacting, Phoenix Magic's gift for self-examination would make it a good choice. If you are writing an article or preparing a speech, you will want the ability to attract recognition for your ideas that Illumination Magic provides and employ the power of persuasion that is Void Magic. If you are trying to heal your body or ground the energy of a group of people and get them to calm down, Healing Touch would be very effective.

Review the vision you created. What magic would be best suited to creating each of the elements in this vision? Chances are, you will need more than one magic. The reason is that most visions are like jigsaw puzzles composed of various pieces that fit together to form a coherent picture. For example, if your vision is to build your practice as a therapist, this vision is composed of elements such as office space, clients, the nature of the therapy you will employ, training to become that kind of therapist, and so on. These elements may have sub-elements within them. For example, you may want a certain type of client, one who is open and willing to make necessary changes, someone who resonates with the work that you do, and who can afford to pay for your services.

What is the higher purpose of what you are trying to create? If it is your vision for a relationship, it may be that you are trying to create a relationship so that you can give and receive unconditional love. Perhaps you want resources so that you can build a counseling practice and help others heal their emotional wounds. Perhaps you want a vacation so that the rest and recreation you receive will help you express more creativity in the job that you do. If you need new clothes, your purpose may be to have garments that better support your life and work. Define a purpose, keeping in mind that you are creating a structure the energy will follow to fruition.

When you create with alchemy, you state the power of the magic you are using and the higher purpose you intend for this creation-event. For example, if your vision is for financial independence, you might use the following statement: *I have the power to transform my financial flow so that it fully upholds my life and spiritual work.*

You can see from this example that you begin with the power of Phoenix Magic, the power to transform. Your vision for financial independence is the focus for this power, and the higher purpose is to create a flow of resources that fully uphold you. As you make the statement of power and purpose, notice how this thought makes you feel. Use the upwelling sense of confidence in your power by channeling this feeling into your heart center. From your crown center at the top of your head, imagine that you are bringing in the energy of co-creation that the Creator always makes available to you in the present moment. Channel this co-creative force into your heart center, bringing it together with the power you feel while you state your desire for essence. You might use the following statement:

> *I desire joy, creativity, ease, fun, financial freedom, and an abundant flow of resources that supports my spiritual journey.*

Then release the energy from your heart center, sending it to all corners of the universe. If your vision is to create a new job or profession, there are several approaches you could take. If you wanted to transform your career into something higher, you might use the power of Phoenix Magic and use the following statement:

> *I have the power to transform my career into to one that truly reflects who I am as Spirit.*

If you simply wanted to attract a new job, you might choose Sex Magic and use the following statement:

I have the power to attract a job that supports my highest good.

Whatever your vision may be, it is crucial that you remove your attention from any desired forms that inspired your essence words. Instead, focus completely on the essence of what you are trying to create. When you are choosing essence words, start with the spiritual essences that matter most to you, like joy, creativity, ease, freedom, fun, unconditional love, and contribution to healing the planet. If you are creating a soulmate relationship, for example, here are some essence words that might be appropriate:

I desire joy, creativity, ease, unconditional love, and a deeply committed, heart-centered relationship filled with warmth, fun, mutual respect and support, with a partner who resonates with my vision and who can readily share my spiritual path.

If you are creating a new car, you might want to use the following essences:

I desire joy, creativity, ease, freedom, fun, and a vehicle that is reliable, comfortable and economical, that I can use for both work and recreation.

Remember that you are creating a structure, a kind of spiritual DNA that will give a framework to co-creative energy as it coalesces into form.

Meditation for Creating with Personal Magic

Take a deep breath and enter the void. Invite all limiting thoughts and feelings into the void to be released to their higher evolution. State the power of the magic you are using by saying to yourself, "I have the power to…", finishing the statement with the power of the magic you have chosen. Then declare the higher purpose of what you are creating. These statements should evoke an emotional response that you can feel as energy. Direct this energy into your heart center. Then, imagine you are bringing down from your crown center and into your heart the energy that the Creator has made available to you for co-creating with Spirit. As these two energies meet, you will sense a subtle building sensation in your heart center. When this happens, state your desire for essence by saying, "I desire joy, creativity, ease…" and whatever other essences you are trying to create. When you are finished, allow the

energy to leave your heart center and move out to all dimensions in the universe
while you say, "I have spoken, and it is so!"

Higher purpose helps Spirit know the reason you want something so that it can inform what you create with your purposeful intent. In other words, if you ask for money, but you are not clear about what it is for, Spirit is not likely to respond. This is because money is simply a means of exchange that has no meaning in the Spirit realm. If your purpose for the money is to make you feel secure because you are afraid of the future, Spirit will not respond because to do so would rob you of your lessons about staying in present time. Spirit does not hear the half-truth of wants born of fear, ego, or neediness because these are the language of Mind. This does not mean that you cannot ask for financial resources. It simply means that the essence of what you want to create is probably not the money itself, but what you hope to buy with the money. If you ask for financial freedom, Spirit can easily interpret this language and respond accordingly.

When you state the power of the magic you are using, you become aware that you really *do* have that power. That power, no matter what the magic, is a gift of Spirit and is therefore within you. Stating the power of a magic invokes that magic and makes its energy available for co-creation. When you declare a purpose, you inform Spirit of your intention. And when you state your desire for essence, you provide information about the essential nature of what you are creating so that the forms Spirit brings you will produce the essence you desire in your heart.

Essence is the language of Spirit, and when you speak your desire for essence, you provide a powerful focus for alchemical energy. The moment you provide this structure, form begins to coalesce around the essence, and what is birthed into being is something that resonates with you as Spirit. When you create from essence, you are asking that the desires of the soul be energized and birthed into being. You transcend the limiting matrix of your thought-forms, and in so doing, shift the matrix into alignment with Spirit. When you do this, you *change* your agreement with the universe about what your reality will be!

If you react to the creating exercise with doubt, you may want to release both judgment and doubt into the void and work on your matrix. Then do the creation exercise again. If you do the exercise and find that the statement of power and purpose do not stir your emotions, then your true purpose may not be what you think, and there may be fear that needs to be invited into the void. Your hesitation might also indicate that the magic you have chosen is not appropriate. It could be that there are sub-elements you have not identified or that are not well aligned with the magic you are using, even though the magic you have chosen seems quite appropriate to your greater vision.

If you are creating a complex project or vision, the use of multiple magics will make creating more effortless. For example, if you are creating a trip to promote your business, you will need to look at the elements. You may want to use Void Magic to help you plan your itinerary and make decisions about where you should go and whom you should meet. You may want to use Sex Magic to attract the resources to pay for your travel expenses. You would probably use Illumination Magic to create your sales pitch, your marketing materials, and audio-visual aids for your presentation. You might use Sacred Weaving to connect your clients with the energy and higher purpose of your mutual endeavor, or to create sacred space in which the client can be honest and forthcoming about his concerns. Time Magic might help you identify opportunities that become spontaneously available to you and allow you to observe subtle signals that might alert you to hidden agendas in the transaction. If you find yourself in the middle of a negotiation that is stalled, you may want to use Healing Touch to move the energy of fear and transform it. If the results of your trip are disappointing, you may want to use Stillness Magic to assist you in finding the spiritual gift the situation has for you. You might then use Phoenix Magic to examine what happened and to assist you in transforming what needs to shift.

If you review your vision and you see areas that are blurry or that do not seem to have much energy, this is probably an indication that an element or sub-element needs to be created to complete the picture. If your vision is something that makes you sigh and does not ignite your enthusiasm, examine the vision for essence. Is this a vision that has essence for you? If it does not, this vision may no longer be your authentic dream. If it does have essence, release any beliefs you have that this vision is too grand or unrealistic, then set about energizing what you want to create. Bring the essences you desire into your life in small ways. If you want beauty, give attention to anything beautiful in your environment. If you want joy, find a way to do things that make you joyful, like listening to your favorite music or feeding the birds. If the form of your vision is not clear to you, then focus entirely on essence and trust that the forms this brings you will satisfy your heart's desire.

While desire for essence always occurs in present time, timing is often an influence upon creation-events. The universe works like a clockwork, with gears upon gears whose cogs intersect perfectly in the fullness of time. If a form does not seem to be coming to you in the time you expect, discard your schedule. Some forms require the interaction with people and events, each with their own engagement with fruition. Know that your magic is working and that Spirit is upholding you. When co-creative energy matures in the structures you have designed, the timing will make itself apparent, and fruition will result in a creation-event that gives you essence.

Magic has great power to create what you want, but it is not about controlling the future. It is about creating the life you want in the now. There are no alchemical possibilities in any time other than the moment in which you find yourself. The secret to alchemy is to remain rooted in the now and to refuse to leave it. The instant you move from the moment and become anxious about the future or concerned about the past, magic and your ability to perform alchemy are lost to you. If you are self-centered in your request, your purpose will not be a higher one. If you are dwelling on the past, you will try to create from resisting what has already been created in the universe. If you are fearful about the future, you will try to create from avoiding what you fear. In any case, you will not be in present time where the power of magic is accessible to you.

How often should you do these exercises? Taking things to the void should be done on a minute-by-minute basis as you recognize unwanted thoughts and feelings that come up throughout your day. Transmuting feelings should be done any time you are aware of a fear. Matrix work should be done daily for three to five minutes. Creating can also be done once a day. When you sense that your dream has changed, update your vision or create a new one. As each exercise is repeated over the course of many days, take care to give it your full attention so that it does not become an empty ritual that you do automatically, without feeling it.

When you use alchemy, you are taking action to influence creation-events in your life. The reason is that when you are creating with alchemy, you are living in authenticity and in the full expression of gifts that Spirit has made available to you. Your birthright is joy, creativity, and ease. Alchemy is the key to living that birthright.

Creating with alchemy is about manifesting the only things that truly matter: the things that come to you through your connection to Spirit. When you live in a state of love and joy through your connection to the Creator, you are inspired by this heart connection to dance with the Creator and co-create with Spirit. It is then that you come to understand what you are here to do: to approach each day with willingness and intention to co-create the day in present time. Then, and only then, can life become a beautiful dance of joy, lived from your heart to the heart of the Creator. Allow the Creator to be spontaneous with you and bring you forms that you might never have expected. Know that, whatever the form, the Creator's only wish is to bring you essence in great abundance.

APPENDIX

Essence Words

Being States

joy	strength	openness
creativity	perseverance	simplicity
ease	lightness of being	adventure
freedom	clarity	serendipity
unconditional love	healing	integrity
beauty	wholeness	honesty
inspiration	innocence	balance
divinity	patience	understanding
flow	release	abundance
mobility	surrender to Spirit	connection
compassion	transformation	contribution
generosity	faith	peace
devotion	willingness	serenity
imagination	humility	satisfaction
spontaneity	insight	fortitude
trust	flexibility	well-being
higher guidance	detachment	community
brotherhood	gentleness	resonance
sisterhood	communication	independence
family of humankind	fun	fairness
knowledge	wisdom	equality
courage	grace	enlightenment

Circumstances

financial freedom	excellent health	balanced lifestyle
soulmate relationship	Soulful work	loving friends
empowering colleagues	spiritual community	service of higher good

Objects & Surroundings

reliable	beautiful	warm
dependable	durable	sunny
supports my work	practical	cool
supports my health	easy-care	pleasing to my senses
privacy	low-maintenance	effortless
contact with Nature	economical	restful
stimulation	luxurious	peaceful
quiet	eco-friendly	reflects my wholeness
animal-friendly	comfortable	reflects my authenticity
comfortable	cozy	inviting

Interactions

unconditionally loving	supportive	generosity of Spirit
kind	considerate	respectful
honoring	valuing	easy to be with
joyful	accepting	reciprocal
playful	understanding	passionate
liberating	honest	authentic

0-595-29318-2